D1263838

You've Got to Learn
Because I've Got to Teach

YOU'VE GOT TO LEARN BECAUSE I'VE GOT TO TEACH

Bob Sorgi

LIBRARY

Court House Square Press
Hanford, California
1988

© 1988 by Bob Sorgi.
All rights reserved.
Printed in the
United States of America

*No part of this book may be reproduced or transmitted in any form
or by any means electronic or mechanical, including photocopying,
recording or by any information storage and retrieval system,
without the written permission of the copyright owner,
except for brief quotations embodied in reviews.*

Library of Congress Cataloging-in-Publication Data
Sorgi, Robert, 1932—
You've got to learn because I've got to teach
ISBN 0-944248-03-9 : $15.95
1. Sorgi, Robert, 1932—   .
2. Elementary school teachers—
United States—Biography.
I. Title.
LA2317.S635A3 1988
372.11'092'4--dc19
88—15052
CIP

PUBLISHED BY

COURT HOUSE SQUARE PRESS
1231 North Harris
Hanford, California 93230

LA
2317
S635
A3
1988

Contents

To Sue, Annie and Ronnie.

Foreword

Bob Sorgi's delightful story of his experiences as an elementary school teacher validates a conclusion I reached during my four-decade career as a professional educator—some people are born to be teachers. After reading *You've Got To Learn Because I've Got To Teach*, I am convinced that Sorgi is one of them. His expression of the sheer joy of playing a positive role in the growth and development of young children reflects a refreshing ray of hope in an enterprise which has had more than its share of uncertainties.

I have often said that no one goes into teaching to become rich unless he or she is the victim of some bad counseling. I was wrong for it is clear that this educator has accumulated a degree of wealth that is beyond measure.

He believes that discipline, enthusiasm, love, motivation, patience, and a sense of humor are among the behaviors that must be brought into play if effective teaching is to be achieved. Yet, these qualities are seldom included among recommendations emanating from current studies to improve the quality of teaching in the nation's schools. Policymakers would do well to examine *You've Got To Learn Because I've Got To Teach* if they wish to add some reality to the theories on which they are being urged to act. One reality would be to discover more Bob Sorgis and encourage and support them to teach our children.

WILSON RILES

Preface

I don't like teaching. I *love* it! The thought of having embarked on any other career is unthinkable. Retirement? The word itself is offensive to me. Would a golf addict voluntarily retire from the links? Can you imagine a fisherman, who revels in the pursuit of the elusive trout, hanging up his lures at anything but gunpoint? But, you say, teaching is a job, not recreation. Wouldn't you like to quit working and do all the fun things you've always dreamed of doing? In answer to that question I'd reply, For me, teaching is a game. It gives me such joy that it *is* recreation! Besides, with so much vacation time, I can still indulge in all sorts of recreation—like throwing and catching a football, playing softball, building model planes and boats, travel—you name it.

Strangely enough, I fell into the profession of teaching almost by accident. As a result of being raised at a time when aviators were bigger-than-life supermen, I envisioned myself as an intrepid, globe-encircling pilot, calling such places as Cairo, Rome, London, Singapore and Buenos Aires home. Only because of a severe lack of directional sense did I decide, for the sake of all concerned, to forgo entering the field of commercial aviation. Without the slightest exaggeration, only twice during the day can I tell direction with any degree of certitude: at sunrise and at sunset. On a cloudy day, forget it! It cracks me up whenever people give me directions such as, Head north. At the third traffic light go west. I would much prefer, Go straight ahead. Hang a left at the third light.

Some might ask, Why such a wordy title? For this I can "blame" Jesse Jackson. After reading an article in a San Francisco newspaper in which Mr. Jackson was quoted as having said that a teacher's attitude ought to be, "You've got to learn because I've got to teach," I couldn't help feeling, Hey, that's me! Basically (a word that is currently being beaten to a pulp), I like to talk ... no question about it. Even without Jesse Jackson's influence, the title would probably have been lengthy.

Hopefully, readers will derive an appropriate amount of pleasure while poring through the pages of this book ... enough, at least, to compensate for depriving themselves of other diversions. Finding life too serious to be taken seriously, I adopted a lighthearted approach. Which reminds me of two songwriting brothers I knew years ago back in The Bronx. Their songs may have been forgettable but their business card was definitely worth remembering. It declared with pride: Rejected by the Best!

This book was begun in Salinas and completed in Hanford—both in California. As I bring it to a conclusion, I'd like to express my gratitude to my wife, Sue, for her constructive criticism and sparkling suggestions while wading through the 60,000-plus-word manuscript. It's hard for me to imagine anyone having been more easygoing, yet efficient, while enduring so taxing a task. Our thinking is similar to the point that almost 100 percent of the changes Sue recommended were implemented—quickly—with my wholehearted approval!

My Aunt Mary and mother-in-law, Iva, provided much-needed assistance: Aunt Mary as a grammarian of considerable erudition, and Iva, for stating with supposedly uncharacteristic kindness for a mother-in-law, that the book was "getting better all the time."

Lest I forget, our smoothly functioning air conditioning apparatus was instrumental in allowing me to work through the San Joaquin Valley's dog days of July and August, during which time the thermometer seemed to demonstrate an addiction for readings above 100 degrees.

Last, but certainly not least, I must thank our five kitty-cats for teaching me patience. It's not every cat-owning writer who'd let sleeping cats lie—on his notes—just when he needed them the most!

BOB SORGI
Hanford, California
November 2, 1986

Chapter One

Basically Me

"Sorgi, someday you're going to be a millionaire!" I wondered what could have prompted the speech professor to make such a prediction in front of a class of future teachers. Perhaps it was my gift of gab, a flair for the dramatic, and lots of enthusiasm. Surely some of this enthusiasm was due to my being the only guy in many of my classes. After attending classes composed solely of boys for twelve years, the change was delightful!

That prediction did wonders for my ego, allowing me to float through the rest of the day's classes, clearly visualizing my future home: English Tudor, of course; rustic setting, naturally; Westchester County would do. I had been given a thought to build a dream on and my dream was getting more elaborate by the minute. That million dollars was already burning a hole in my pocket. But for the life of me, I couldn't imagine how either of the two careers I was considering could provide me with such earning power!

Flying had always intrigued me so I enrolled in college, planning to stay only the two years then required for admission to a military flight school. Teaching also was very appealing and sounded practical just in case my "flight plan" didn't work out for whatever reason. This much I knew: if I ever taught school, I'd try to create an atmosphere in which

1

my students would feel relaxed and eager to learn. For the sake of good communication and discipline my motto would be: Say what you mean and mean what you say! And certainly there would be lots of laughs and methods of making the subject matter interesting, no matter what the subject.

I was raised in the north Bronx, the son of pharmacists who ran a good, old-fashioned corner drugstore with an atmosphere similar to that of a country store. During the '30s, it even had a potbellied stove. Friends would gather at the store and all sorts of topics were discussed, ranging from classical music, which could always be heard in the background, to Italy's little war with Ethiopia, and later, the battles of World War II. It was a place where customers sometimes unloaded their heartaches, and my parents were willing listeners, rendering whatever consolation they could. Among the old customers, many a tear was shed when Andrew and Rose Sorgi decided to retire. My brother, John, my sister, Mary, and I had chosen other careers, so the business was sold.

My father, Andrew Sorgi, had immigrated to the United States from Sicily in 1898 as a ten-year-old with his parents and younger brother, Charles. Grandfather Sorgi was a stone cutter. It was always fascinating to hear my father talk about New York City without cars, and of his first big impression, the parade for conquering hero Admiral Dewey.

Pop had studied briefly for the priesthood, then given up these studies after the death of Grandmother Sorgi. He never showed any particular interest in pharmacy. When I once asked him why he chose pharmacy as a career, the reason he gave me was that he had studied Latin in the seminary and this gave him a good background for the study of pharmacy. Besides, it was a short course. "What else could I do?" he'd said. Well, he spent almost fifty years in a profession he wasn't interested in. Furthermore, he didn't even believe in medicines!

My father was a poet at heart, a romanticist who wrote poetry in both English and Italian. He also had a deep love for classical music and wrote a book on his hero, composer Johannes Brahms. It took him eight years to write that book, working into the wee hours of the morning.

My mother, Rose Ferro, was a red-haired Sicilian who immigrated to the United States in 1906 with her parents, four brothers and a sister. Grandfather Ferro was a doctor. As a youngster in Sicily he had watched entranced as Garibaldi's army marched through his village. Feeling a sudden surge of patriotism, he asked one of the soldiers if he could join them. He was promptly told to go home to his baby bottle. He had preceded the family to the United States, studied English super-arduously and managed, at the age of sixty, to pass the New York State examination for medical doctor. Grandmother Ferro had come from a wealthy family but financial reverses had eliminated that wealth. The marriage of my maternal grandparents was one of those arranged deals, for she loved another. Besides, he was fifteen years her senior. But it sure worked. There was a total of ten children!

My mom wanted to be a doctor but that privilege went to her brother, Anthony, who wanted to be an engineer. Instead, Mom got to be a pharmacist along with her brother, Edward, who couldn't have cared less about pharmacy.

There's an interesting bit of irony in this otherwise simple immigration story. My Uncle Ed, who arrived on Ellis Island as an eleven-year-old Sicilian immigrant and became an unhappy pharmacist, in later years obtained a position with the United States Immigration Service and rose to the rank of Chief Inspector of Immigration on Ellis Island! His brother, Joe, who came to America at the tender age of five, studied engineering, rising to the position of New York City's Commissioner of Buildings.

Mom worked as a pharmacist for many years but her special talents were sewing and arts and crafts. As a young woman she had had the opportunity of earning a high salary as a dress designer but shied away from this career because she felt, at the time, that her knowledge of English wasn't adequate.

Looking back on my boyhood days in The Bronx, I always associate classical music with the start of a school day. The first composer who comes to mind is Haydn, since each morning at eight o'clock, just as I was waking up, WQXR opened its morning program with his Clock Symphony.

While I'd be stumbling out of bed, Mom would be exhorting Pop to hurry, claiming that he was opening the store later each day. What would the customers think? With the music of Mozart, Schumann and other musical giants providing a melodious background and my parents carrying on a lively "discussion" as to the proper time for a business to open its doors, I'd get ready for another day of school.

I rarely expected school to be fun. I couldn't imagine it as being anything other than a necessary penance levied on children due to the fall of Adam. There must have been some days when I looked forward to school but I'm hard pressed to remember many. This is not to say that the good nuns poisoned my existence. It is to say that I much preferred being outdoors, far from the restrictions of the classroom. What I definitely found least attractive was the threat of corporal punishment. Although there were no bloodbaths, I did get my comeuppance on a few occasions. But the nuns could teach and you did learn!

During my eight years of attendance at Saint Frances of Rome School I encountered only one teacher who couldn't control the class. Utter chaos was sometimes the result. Poor thing—she should never have been in teaching.

The regimented classroom was what I grew up with and therefore considered perfectly normal. There was absolutely no talking in class. When a student was given permission to ask a question, he was also required to stand up. During a question-and-answer period, the impression was one of jack-in-the-box. Who pops up here! Who pops up there! Getting up from one's seat and going to another part of the room without permission was equivalent to a felony, and almost unheard of. And showing any signs of irritation at a teacher was virtually a capital offense! (I don't remember even one such instance.)

Recess? This was recess. Line up outside the classroom, go to the lavatory, get a drink at the water fountain, and then return to said classroom to await the resumption of class after the last boy had returned. Talking in a whisper was permitted in the room during recess. That was recess—no running around, no ball playing—just continued restraint. Time involved? Hard to imagine more than fifteen minutes. Physical education? You've got to be kidding! I loved sports and would have been thrilled silly at the chance of playing ball during school hours. But that was not to be. On a handful of occasions, down through the years, we were taken to the gym as a reward for heaven-knows-what and allowed to play dodgeball using a medicine ball. I was so overwhelmed with joy and enthusiasm I could hardly contain myself. And, oh yes, I do recall Friday afternoon movies once in a while.

Searching back in my memory for specific recollections of elementary school, both pleasant and unpleasant, I found it quite difficult to come up with many. Such was the lack of excitement, the sameness of each day, year in and year out.

Here's something different. On one entirely unforgettable day in second grade, I was forced to go to school on *Saturday* morning with a few other unfortunates for extra help in arithmetic. No kid would be apt to forget such an event. It's my only memory of second grade.

"Sorgi, you clown!" Those are the exact words of my fourth grade teacher as a stream of rocks rolled down a hill near my school, threatening to engulf her. The rock slide was the result of my chasing a ball down this hill which was strewn with good-sized boulders. I even greeted her with an innocent, "Hello, Sister," as she nimbly dodged her way to safety. That just about takes care of my fourth grade memories.

My eighth grade teacher, Sister Mary Benigna, was the best teacher I ever had. I couldn't have made such a statement at the time because school was a torment to be endured—a colossal pain throughout the entire body. How could anything concerning it be termed "best?" Is there a "best" tornado?

Sister was strict—on rare occasions even resorting to corporal punishment. On one particular day, I was the object of her wrath. Normally, if a boy's behavior became less than tolerable, he was first invited into the hall. This procedure provided a cooling-off period for Sister, while helping the offender save face during the ensuing fireworks. Punishment consisted of a scolding, sometimes accompanied by a stinging slap in the face. In any case, a kid's day was ruined after such an encounter.

My problem was the result of not copying notes that Sister had written on the blackboard. The kid sitting behind me, Ron Romagnoli, a bosom buddy, had silently warned me that I was flirting with doom. But with a show of bravado, I merely snickered, "What, me worry?" Well, Sister started checking each kid's notebook beginning with the first row. Naturally, I started writing furiously. When she reached me, Sister could readily see that I had just begun copying the notes. There was no invitation into the hall to weigh the matter—no cooling-off period, just instant action. She flattened me on the spot! I didn't exactly adore her for inflicting this punishment on me, but whatever resentment there may have been at the time was of short duration.

If someone were to ask me why I chose Sister Mary Benigna as the best of all my teachers, I couldn't rave about any one quality she had. Besides, she tended to favor the brightest students, as was the case with all the other teachers. This meant that I apparently was outside her charmed circle, being merely an A-minus student, at best.

But I visited that nun many times after leaving elementary school. I even remember confiding in her after having graduated from college, and didn't get the impression that she was looking down her nose at me for having been other than a straight A student. Sixteen years after leaving her class, I paid her the ultimate compliment. I was on my honeymoon, visiting New York from California, where I now lived. I remembered Sister and took my new bride to meet her, but she wasn't in town. That was a long time ago, so Sister must now be either retired or gone to her reward.

Ah, but life wasn't made up of only school. There were plenty of fun times.

The north Bronx of my youth had much in the way of open spaces. Parts of it were even quite heavily wooded. But what really attracted my friends and me was the Bronx River, to which we always seemed to gravitate when not engaged in a hotly contested game of stickball, New York City's favorite street sport.

This river, although very picturesque, was also incredibly polluted! I mean sewage of the human waste variety could actually be seen floating in places. Nevertheless, some diehard kids with obviously Spartan constitutions managed to muster up enough courage to bathe in these filthiest of waters. But I don't recall even one instance of hearing the beckoning call, Come on in, the water's just fine!

I recall being told that trout had been planted in the river. I also recall hearing that they perished instantly, probably quite happily, considering the alternative.

One novel activity of ours consisted of trying to bop huge water rats on their heads with long sticks. Despite our harassment, these rats all managed to live full and productive lives.

Right by the river were the tracks of the New York, New Haven and Hartford Railroad. We frequently ended up playing by these tracks. Now this could be dangerous, if for no other reason than that the trains ran on electricity. The tracks included a third rail which carried a deadly electrical current. True, this rail had a wooden covering but it wouldn't have been too difficult to accidentally catch one's foot under this covering while stepping over the rail, which stood about a foot above the tracks. Electrocution would have been the result.

One day a friend and I were "goofing off" by the tracks just below the 238th Street Bridge, a huge structure resembling a Roman aqueduct. A drunk who just happened to look down at the tracks while staggering across the bridge spotted us and, for some unknown reason, started cautioning us about the danger of electrocution. My friend took this as a golden opportunity to scare this good, but incoherent, Samaritan out of his inebriated wits. The drunk had been specifically warning us not to touch the third rail. Ron made it appear that he intended doing precisely the opposite, even asking him where it would be best to touch the deadly rail.

The scene that followed is vividly etched in my mind: the poor guy screaming at the top of his lungs, "Don't touch it, you'll get killed!"; Ron repeatedly asking him where he should make contact, at the same time holding his hand ever closer to it, and my laughing hysterically. This experience may have been fun for us but it probably was frightening enough to be truly sobering for the drunk!

Ask any kid from the north Bronx of yesteryear about games he played in his youth, and you're sure to hear some mention of "guns." This game was usually in the form of cops and robbers or cowboys and Indians, with minor variations here and there, of course. Did we have fun? You bet we did!

It must have been extremely funny for any adults or older kids privileged to have been within both seeing and hearing range of these melodramatic, spur-of-the-moment productions. Imagine someone insisting that you were dead, while you argued both vehemently and vociferously that you were, on the contrary, very much alive! After all, how could the bullet have hit you while you were firmly and securely planted behind a rock or a tree?

How unsophisticated and delightfully innocent we must have appeared while running around slapping our thighs, pretending to be cowboys and Indians! Another amusing scene to have witnessed would have been that of the "FBI agent," a cigarette in the form of a short twig dangling rakishly from his lips while he questions a suspect.

One of my friends went about the game of guns very scientifically, producing paraphernalia for our games which were quite fancy, such as handcuffs and binoculars. Sadly, in real life this very nice guy got to know the violence of real guns, for he was killed in action in Korea—ironically, just before he was due to return to the States. Too bad the guns in his life couldn't have been limited to make-believe.

I always enjoyed baseball in its various forms. As a youngster I played softball, stickball, slapball, punchball and "mush." All of these were variations on the main theme. Oh yes, occasionally we did have games of baseball, pure and unadulterated.

What I'll do now is turn back the clock, briefly, to a day in June of 1946. I can see it now ... quite clearly. Just as if four decades had suddenly vanished, there's a group of kids standing on the corner of 236th Street and Byron Avenue. They appear to be organizing a game of mush, one of those adulterated versions of baseball. Let's see. There's Jo-Jo Solitario sporting a crewcut and Ronnie "Rome" swinging a stickball bat. Lo and behold ... Irving Goldsmith is warming up. Oh boy, that guy produces vapor trails with each pitch! And there I am also warming up, throwing so hard it appears I may end up pitching my arm along with the ball. There isn't a chance I'll be able to match Irving's speed, though.

Sides have been picked. It's to be Ronnie and me against Irving and Jo-Jo. Gee, look at that hollow, pink rubber ball being used—a Spaldeen. I'd almost forgotten they existed. Wow, there's only a distance of about fifty feet from the pitcher's mound to the plate. Getting a hit off Irving should be quite an accomplishment. Maybe I'll just put the stickball bat in front of the plate and one of Irving's deliveries will simply rocket off the bat, hitting the wall of my Uncle Ed's house 150 feet away for a triple. If I could only manage to park it over the roof for a homer! What a monumental task, with this human cannon as my adversary. Guess I'll be lucky just to make contact with the ball for a little, dinky single. I'd better quit while I'm still ahead. Over and out ... back to reality.

Regarding my attendance at Cardinal Hayes High School in The Bronx—just getting there was an accomplishment in itself! Having lived almost next door to Saint Frances of Rome School, I was disconcerted by being obliged to endure, over a four-year period, what amounted to more than thirty days of travel on that electrified, mechanized brute of a conveyance known as the subway. Whoever was responsible for introducing mankind to this wheeled beast must have been the ultimate masochist!

And I was one of the more fortunate of subway users because I happened to board the thing at 233rd Street. Because of this station's location near the northern terminus of the Interborough Rapid Transit System—the IRT—I was always able to get a seat on what would resemble, by the time Pelham Parkway was reached, a rolling sardine cannery. Upon arriving at my destination, the 149th Street and Grand Concourse subway station, so great was the density of humanity in each car that the skills of a brilliant fullback were required to gain exit. Can I ever forget the morning when "G" and I, unable to snake or bull our way to the door through the crush of people, actually considered exiting through a window?

The course that left the greatest impression on me while at Hayes was American Literature. Ever hear of a course that taught itself? Well, this one did. The textbook provided a wonderland of adventure, introducing me to such unforgettable stories as, "To Build a Fire," by Jack London, "Footfalls," by Wilbur Daniel Steele, "Flight," by John Steinbeck, and a host of other thrillers. If this course had been taught by a superior teacher, the excitement probably would have been too much for me to handle! Nonetheless, my American Literature teacher lives on in my school recollections for one particular reason. For those students who were so unmotivated as to neglect doing their homework, he had swift and painful punishment consisting of a quick, well-aimed kick in the shins, accompanied by a look of sheer fury. Yet, after school and especially at fun things like skating parties, he was just beautiful—a real nice guy.

At a seemingly unimportant senior assembly, on a day that would normally have been long since forgotten, I was privileged to hear a speaker whose influence in my life was to become paramount. Dr. Loritain, a prominent New York

City educator, was the guest speaker. I can't recall whether I'd ever seriously considered teaching as a career, but by the time this scholarly gentleman had enumerated the benefits derived from teaching, I was quite interested. What appealed to me most was the opportunity to help shape character. I guess I'd been kind of carrying a torch for teaching without being aware of it. Dr. Loritain's talk fanned the flame. But teaching still had to compete with flying, and flying was a hard act to follow. Oh, the thrill of seeing and hearing a squadron of jets roaring across the skies—total ecstasy! And what about those snazzy uniforms, along with the unlimited travel opportunities! Sure, flying was a hard act to follow but providentially, Dr. Loritain's wonderful talk led to my enrollment at Fordham University's School of Education. This move gave me time to "come down to earth." My chosen field of study was elementary education. As a result, I found myself feeling somewhat like a member of a sorority. Not a single other male in the School of Education showed interest in teaching at the elementary level.

Now just how did a future elementary school teacher learn how to teach? Well, first of all, liberal doses of "methods and materials" courses were provided. These courses familiarized the future teacher with the various methods and materials used in the teaching of elementary school subjects. They were helpful but dry, no substitute for actually instructing a class of your own. That chance was afforded the future teacher in senior year. All the future teachers, that is, except me! It was my own fault, really.

To be eligible to practice-teach, a student teacher had to complete a course in speech and diction. I had long since taken the course, passed the written part, but failed on a number of occasions to convince the speech professor that my diction was acceptable. As a result, the course couldn't be considered complete and my grade was listed as incomplete. Now, to graduate I had to pass the diction exam sooner or later. If it had been sooner—like before the beginning of senior year—permission to practice-teach would have been granted me. But instead, I had decided to postpone attempting to pass this most essential examination until later, finally passing diction just before the end of my senior year. And why had I acted so foolishly? Very simple. I'd gotten cold feet. The thought of teaching a class of kids with a teacher as an observer was more than I could handle at the time.

The difficulty I had encountered in passing diction was primarily the result of my having a New York accent. Please don't misunderstand me. I never said "foist" for first, or "boids" instead of birds. And I didn't sound like Fred Flintstone, either. It was just "too New York," whatever that meant. That's kind of humorous—a New Yorker being handicapped by having a New York accent while attending a school in the heart of New York City. Can you imagine a Texan having trouble passing a diction exam at the University of Texas because of a Texas accent?

Having intended to complete two years of college and then, hopefully, qualify for military flight school, I had, instead, continued with my college education and kept my feet planted on the ground, at least temporarily. So, on finishing school I graduated with a bachelor of science degree in education—a rare major in those days for a male.

Now the problem was finding a teaching position. One serious handicap was my lack of practice teaching. It most definitely limited my opportunities. But eventually I landed a teaching job at Saint Jerome's School in the south Bronx. Salary? The grandiose amount of $125 a month—a rather humble beginning for a future "millionaire." The neighborhood was the *Blackboard Jungle* type but the school was the same kind that I had attended—parochial. Therefore and in conclusion, kids behaved or else. The boys were, of course, separated from the girls, and were instructed, for the most part, by brothers, the male equivalent of sisters.

My first class was a fifth grade composed of forty-two boys—as mixed a group, ethnically and racially, as only a melting pot like New York could produce. Because I had chickened out of practice teaching, I now had to face the class cold, without any teaching experience whatsoever. And surprisingly enough, it was a cinch, even though this position was most demanding.

Having gone to parochial school, I was well acquainted with the entire routine. One much-needed change had taken place. Somewhere along the line, an enlightened soul had come to the realization that keeping children cooped up inside a building for hours at a time wasn't pedagogically sound. The idea had been promoted that, in addition to a bathroom break and a drink of water, children should have the chance to go outside and scream, chase one another, play games or just sit and talk with classmates.

As a result of this sound philosophy, a real recess period had been established. It was therapeutic for both kids and teachers. During my own parochial school days, the thought of going outside for recess had never even occurred to me. Now, as a teacher, I saw it not only as a necessity for the children but positively mandatory for the teacher. How else could *he* get a bathroom break? And what about the chance for a cup of coffee or a smoke? In those days I smoked, and looked forward most earnestly to a cigarette at recess. Without a break I would have had nicotine fits as if they were going out of style!

Well, under these more relaxed conditions, it was easier for kids to like school than before. During recess and lunch breaks, I almost always found time to play ball with the kids. The playground was the tenement-lined street in front of the school, which was designated a play street and blocked off while students were outdoors. One of the games was simple enough: I would throw a rubber ball high into the air and the kids would attempt to catch it. After doing this several zillion times, it was a miracle I still had an arm left!

This close association with the kids outside the classroom did much to create rapport. The kids and I were buddies. Inside the classroom there was, of course, a change in our relationship. I was there to teach and the kids' job was to learn. And let's face it, learning takes discipline.

Regimentation—it was never referred to as such—was still the order of the day. There were certain rules which had to be adhered to. They were traditional in parochial schools and helped create an orderly classroom environment. The chief rule was that to either speak or move from one's desk, permission had to be asked for and granted. It was asked for by raising a hand and waiting to be acknowledged. As a teacher I accepted the idea of regimentation as perfectly normal, just as I had as a student. Was there any other way to teach or, for that matter, to learn?

My great desire was to make learning fun. I mean *real* fun—as exciting as playing! But, most important, those forty-two kids had to learn because I had to teach! And regimentation was no impediment. It was synonymous with discipline and discipline was a "must." I had vivid memories of my sixth grade teacher chasing herself due to a lack of discipline in her classroom. I didn't intend for this to happen in mine.

Over the years, I've found that among the key ingredients in smooth and effective teaching are love, enthusiasm, motivation, patience, praise, a sense of humor, and the "big D"—discipline. Call it regimentation if you wish. Remove any of the first six and you can still make it as a teacher, although the kids will be missing important dimensions. Eliminate discipline and the whole complexion of the classroom will change radically ... for the worse.

Admittedly, during my first year of teaching, some of the techniques I used for achieving discipline were rather primitive ... and dumb! I shudder when thinking of occasions when I raised my voice loud enough to crack glass, and I'll never forget the time I ordered this little guy (now 40 years old) who had run afoul of the law to make himself scarce by taking up residence in the coat closet. And so who should walk into my room requesting to see said little person but the principal!

As stated earlier, this teaching position was demanding. A teacher was required to follow a syllabus, a guide outlining the material which it was essential to teach. You were not restricted to this subject matter, but if any of it wasn't taught and questions pertaining to it appeared on the final exams that came from the superintendent's office, it could prove embarrassing.

The supervisor's report of a classroom visit included more than seventy items on which you were evaluated. Was the discipline in your room rigid and cold, or cooperative? Did the kids appear alert, happy, interested? Were their study habits good? How did they respond to a quiz on the lesson that was taught during the visit? What was the condition of the students' desks, both inside and out?

Oh yes, the supervisor's report was comprehensive, all right! It took place over a two-day period. I'd been teaching less than three months. As a result, I was really nervous. But at the conclusion of his visit, after I noted the report filled with "V.G.s" signifying very good, my joy knew no bounds. I was especially pleased to know that the kids appeared happy. To top it all off, the supervisor even complimented me on my "zeal and enthusiasm."

Sure, I was enthusiastic. I loved teaching those children and had discovered that my ideas on teaching were practical, and that the kids and I could have lots of laughs both in and out of the classroom without their becoming abusive. Very early in my teaching career, I became aware that I had found my niche. "Sorgi, you *are* a millionaire already," I thought. The speech professor, Mr. Ebbene, had been so right!

Chapter Two

A Quack Quack Here and a Jaguar There

"Mr. Sorgi, do I hear ducks in your room?" The question was directed at me by the very upset housemother, Mrs. Dobson. With a quack quack here and a quack quack there, the ducks were making an ungodly racket. There was no use in trying to deny that my room had become a temporary shelter for ducks. The outraged Mrs. Dobson informed me without a smidgen of tact that my teaching contract included room and board—for me, adding that she couldn't recall any provision for animals, especially the likes of ducks!

The problem had begun at Easter time when I'd joyfully presented my niece and three nephews with half a dozen baby ducks, much to my sister's disgust. She was forever imploring me to keep her children's gifts inanimate. It got so bad that she cringed when the holidays rolled around, wondering what sort of animal would next take up abode in her already-crowded home. My brother-in-law, Tom, merely smiled through it all, realizing that, come what may, the period of occupancy would doubtless be of short duration.

The pattern was always the same: from pet shop to my sister's house and inevitably back to me. At times the cycle would be complete, the pets winding up in the same pet shop from which they'd originated.

Well, the ducks had to go—no question about it. I hustled them out of the room as quickly as possible and penned them up outside until I could con my brother into taking them. After all, he had a farm, and what would a farm be without a few ducks?

Peace had been restored to Marlborough Academy, a private boarding school for boys in a plush New York City suburb. It was owned and operated by an individual who was having a tough time getting his financial act together. The school comprised two Victorian mansions, one considerably larger and more elaborate than the other. They were separated by a wide expanse of lawn and a narrow stretch of woods. The students came from such varied places as Venezuela, Colombia, Canada, and, of course, Brooklyn. For some reason, almost all the kids were Jewish.

Classes were small. After having handled a class of forty-two, this was heavenly. But I was on duty six and a half days a week, with each day beginning at 7:30 A.M. and not ending until 9:30 P.M. So the contrasts between my first two teaching positions were great. Except in salary, which remained at $125 a month. But I enjoyed my new job. It certainly provided me with a wealth of teaching experience.

My class consisted of thirteen students in grades seven and eight. The classroom was in the parlor of the smaller mansion. From the first day of school there existed a situation geared to cause any teacher to climb the walls.

Can you imagine trying to teach thirteen junior high boys seated at two round tables that squeak and rock? Happily, a solution was found through the construction of a couple of long, wooden tables.

The interesting part of this job was trying to get the materials. I was given permission to order whatever supplies were needed from a local lumber company. But the company wasn't deliriously happy at the thought of extending credit to the already overextended owner-headmaster. Such was the school's financial status, at the time.

Yet, the lumber was delivered, and in short order I built the tables, with some "help" from the kids. The headmaster's glee was superseded only by mine.

With its fireplace, piano, and homey bay windows, that parlor made the coziest classroom one could imagine. For the sake of providing pleasant breaks from the ordinary classroom routine, and also as a source of enrichment, I've always read and told my classes an abundance of stories, both fact and fiction.

One unlimited source of fascinating and sometimes spooky stories has been Edward Rowe Snow, New England's famous author of adventure stories relating to the sea. The parlor's setting, especially on stormy days, was perfect for the telling of such Snow classics as "Dr. Winslow's Heart," "The Lady with the Missing Finger," "The Frozen Couple," and many other captivating tales of action and adventure.

That last story was really a "beaut." It concerned a couple who had been lashed together to the mast of a ship that was foundering in a storm along the coast of Maine. The object was to keep them from being washed overboard. As their bodies were splashed by the pounding surf, they gradually became completely encased in ice. The next morning, after the storm had subsided, a rescue party went aboard the ship which, by now, had run aground. They found the couple and, much to their astonishment, discovered signs of life. Ever so carefully, the man and woman were removed from the mast and the ice slowly chopped away. Miraculously, both of them survived!

Recess in this idyllic setting involved an indeterminate amount of time relaxing on the lawn or just sitting on the mansion's steps. I stayed with the kids the whole time and considered it recess for me as well because I was permitted to smoke up a storm with my king-sized cigarettes. This was a liberal policy, indeed. In almost all schools, to this day, teachers who wish to smoke are restricted to a certain area, usually the teachers' lounge.

Today, with fewer and fewer school personnel smoking, lounges are no longer the dire threat to health that they once were. Talk about the proverbial smoke-filled room! I can remember being in teachers' lounges where the smoke was so thick the only safe means of navigation was via instruments. I even heard tell of one unfortunate educator who became so disoriented in the impenetrable haze that he simply vanished, never to be seen or heard of again. (As a friend once told me, "What I like about you, Bob, is ... you never exaggerate!")

Between recesses of impressive length, a most reasonable lunch break, and a sprinkling of exciting stories, I somehow managed to squeeze in science, math, social studies, and language.

There was no shortage of fun for those thirteen kids and me after school. Being obliged to spend almost ninety hours a week together, I'd hate to imagine what life would have been like for us had we not gotten along so well. We played lots of baseball, took walks to the ice cream parlor and yacht harbor, went on a trip to Manhattan for visits to the United Nations and the Museum of Natural History, drove around in my convertible and, in general, enjoyed one another's company. The responsibility of hauling a bunch of kids around off campus didn't faze me in the least. Ah, youth!

One Friday night I took my class to a nearby amusement park, known far and wide as Playland. We were all enjoying ourselves immensely. On one of the rides, called The Hammer, there was room for only two, so I chose to take Milton with me on what I thought of as being an ordinary ride requiring only a minimum of daring.

If memory serves me correctly, The Hammer consisted of a pair of cages, one at each end of a long steel bar. This bar was attached to a mechanism which allowed it to turn on a vertical plane, similar to a windmill. As the bar turned, the cages spun and dove toward the ground. Now Milton imagined himself to be brave, sort of a youthful John Wayne. But on this particular night, Milt learned the meaning of the word *fright*. When the cage we were riding in plunged earthward, Milt cowered down in his seat and began a lament that included, "Mommy, Daddy, help!" This monologue was accompanied by the sound of pocket change flying around the cage as it whirled and spun crazily. The poor kid was so scared ... and so embarrassed. But to his credit, it wasn't long before he settled down and tried to enjoy what remained of the ride. Emerging from the cage, he even managed to laugh about the experience.

Despite the easygoing atmosphere and fun times, earning a mere $125 a month made it imperative that I search for greener educational pastures. Shortly before leaving Marlborough, I experienced a tension-filled episode of brief duration which left me emotionally drained.

Joey was a cute little guy in kindergarten. Now, Joey and I were buddies. He knew I loved him dearly. One night Joey became mysteriously ill, and his father, who happened to be visiting him, began to panic. His first thought was I must get my son to the hospital and fast! But he had no car so, of course, as Joey's special buddy, I was asked to use my car as an ambulance. Too bad it didn't look like one and make ambulance-like sounds. What a ride that was! With Joey's father literally begging me to disregard all traffic signals and speed limits, assuring me that he'd pay any fines I might incur, I somehow maneuvered my way to the hospital, surprisingly not leaving any destruction in my wake. Fortunately, there was nothing seriously wrong with Joey, and a greatly relieved father was only too happy to reward me with a goodly supply of choice cigars for this act "above and beyond the call of duty."

The night before my final day at the academy turned out to be a real winner. I had a few hours off that evening and decided to head for The Bronx and home. While on the Hutchinson River Parkway, I ran out of gas—a favorite habit of mine in those days. Naturally, help wasn't available for a while. At long last, a policeman spotted me, stopped and offered to take me to the nearest gas station. I accepted gladly and was supplied with what might aptly be described as "rapid transit."

Upon telling me that there was a Thunderbird engine under the hood, he proceeded to "floor it" to demonstrate its efficiency. I must have said something inane, like "cool, man" or "jazzy," at the same time thinking of the assortment of traffic tickets I'd probably collect for putting on a demonstration of what I had under *my* car's hood. No big deal, though. All I wanted was some gas. And the gas station was closed! The policeman had his own business to attend to and left me stranded. The only transportation available was either hitchhiking or my size nine-and-a-half feet.

I decided that it was closer to my home than to the school and so began a journey that didn't wind up until the wee hours—like about 4:00 A.M.—since I wasn't able to get any rides.

In the morning I called the headmaster and explained the situation. After being driven to my car with a can of gas, I rushed to school. The kids wondered where I'd been and assured me that the power structure wasn't exactly singing my praises. But *the* power structure himself didn't have a word to say about anything. It was payday and his big problem was paying me my $125 a month salary.

I received my salary all right, but it came in bits and pieces. By the time the headmaster had finished counting out $125, he had long since been reduced to quarters, dimes, nickels ... and even pennies. The poor guy must have been totally mortified. But it was downright embarrassing for me, too, as I accepted a whole mess of coins and stuffed them into my pockets as my hands became filled.

It was only then that I realized how close to bankruptcy the school was. Tenacity, though, was one of the headmaster's strong points. He stuck it out and the school survived through thick and thin for a number of years until at last, for whatever reason, it closed its doors.

Marlborough served its purpose: primarily as a boarding school for boys with problems and also as a place where beginning teachers could get the experience necessary to compete for much better paying jobs with the public school districts. Without a year or two of teaching experience, the chances of being hired by a public school district were slim.

I've never been overly fond of job hunting, nor am I acquainted with anyone who gets his kicks out of messing with resumes or being interviewed, wondering just what the interviewer wants to hear. But that's neither here nor there. I left Marlborough with little experience and no New York State Teaching Certificate, thanks to not having taken student teaching. It was a discouraging task, that's for sure. Besides the standard You don't have enough teaching experience bit, I once—in Westchester County—even got to hear the old refrain about having a New York accent, and just why it wasn't desirable! Oh, that was maddening! I began wondering what made *my* New York accent so distinctive ... and terrible! Certainly, most of the teachers in the New York Metropolitan Area had New York accents and the schools didn't seem to be disintegrating.

At long last, in the latter part of August, I was offered a sixth grade teaching position in a school district in northern Westchester County. The salary was almost 300 percent more than what I'd been earning at Marlborough Academy.

McKinley School, to which I'd been assigned, was located about forty miles north of my Bronx home. This meant that each school day I would spend approximately two hours on the road. But I was a kid and loved to drive, especially when the car was a brand new, midnight blue Jaguar 3.4 sedan with real leather upholstery and a dashboard made of gorgeous wood paneling.

With that car I felt like a capitalist but was paying dearly for the feeling: $120 a month in car payments, which amounted to more than one-third of my monthly gross pay. My reasons for buying the car: first, the convertible I'd been driving looked as if it were in the final stages of becoming an accordion, thanks to a drunk who rear-ended me; and second, that Jag was too beautiful to resist. It would go well with Westchester County. Moreover, hadn't it been predicted that someday I would be a millionaire? Well, now that I had a job that paid more than mere pocket change, I might as well start looking prosperous!

And so the school year began. By some odd chance there was a woman teaching in the school district who lived within a mile or so of my home—really quite a coincidence! She was a commuter. After being introduced to each other we agreed to ride together and share expenses. The gal's name was Jo. She and her husband, Gus, were very happily married. But because he was employed in downtown New York City and her place of work was almost in upstate New York, they were virtual strangers.

Many were the years that Jo had been teaching in this faraway district and loving it. For some reason, though, she had never learned to drive. Hence, an exhaustingly complex daily journey by railroad, bus, and who knows what else. She would have to rise while even the birds were still in the midst of their dreams, and get home at some outrageous hour. And now ... she was being picked up, driven to her school and delivered right back to her very doorstep in a Jaguar sedan! Who said that prayers aren't answered?

The trip to school was not only scenic, but also steeped in American history and folklore. Each day's drive took us over the Headless Horseman Bridge, made famous by Washington Irving in his well-known tale, "The Legend of Sleepy Hollow." We also passed the site where the British spy, Major Andre, was captured during the Revolutionary War. Then there was the majestic Hudson River, not far from the road for most of our journey.

Peekskill, the town in which we taught, was representative of America at mid-century. There were neat frame houses of simple construction as well as ornately designed Victorian homes of great beauty. The streets were tree-lined, and a lovely park near McKinley School added to the peaceful setting.

Jo and I taught in different schools within the same school district. Hers was right by the Hudson and looked like something out of a ghost story—a perfect setting for the Addams Family of television fame. So antique was its appearance that I wonder that I didn't hear the sound of a harpsichord whenever I approached this relic of another age. My school, on the other hand, resembled a stately English mansion, a most impressive elementary school in every sense of the word.

The class to which I was assigned was composed of twenty-eight sixth grade boys and girls. At long last I would be teaching girls! I encountered another significant change. The kids at McKinley School came from a variety of socio-economic and religious backgrounds. This diversity I found stimulating.

Almost all the kids came to school squeaky-clean and ready to learn. They learned plenty that year from current events alone. The biggest news was the launching of Sputnik, an accomplishment that in those days was mind-

boggling. Imagine an object from planet Earth flying around
in outer space! Not nearly as dramatic but, nonetheless, of
great future import, was the emergence of Ghana as a free
African nation. Africa would never be the same again. And,
lo and behold, much to the disgust of King's English lovers,
the word *ain't* was added to the dictionary. That confused
me so much. Ever since entering first grade, I'd heard that
ain't was of such poor quality, grammatically, that it was
almost a bad word. Now it could be used with impunity.
Saints preserve us!

These sixth graders really appreciated humor, so I did
a lot of clowning around. All I had to do to get the kids
in a jovial mood was to bang a pencil on my desk, at the
same time saying, in a horribly squeaky voice, "Now, now,
children, you must behave yourselves!" It cracked me up
to watch them crack up. Once in a while I'd jokingly warn
them that I might someday become a Now, Now, Children
teacher if they didn't do right and mind their p's and q's.
They never appeared too worried that this might happen.

Sometimes, though, the kids would get carried away with
their laughter and I'd have to get grumpy with some of them
to settle them down for classwork. But I considered that a
small price to pay for all the fun we had and the closeness
that developed among us.

As to the subject matter to be taught in class, there
was much freedom. You simply distributed the various textbooks and started on whatever page looked appealing. Page
One always seemed to look good to me and that's where I'd
generally start. And what were the chances of covering all
the material in each subject? If you just wanted to skim
through the books lightly you could finish all the textbooks
from cover to cover. But the kids, including the bright ones,
would retain little.

I've always believed in quality rather than quantity. Before beginning the day's work in social studies, for example,

we'd review yesterday's work and maybe even that of the previous three or four days. It wouldn't take long and would help the kids retain what they'd learned. After asking the class the name of Switzerland's famous mountain range and hearing the word *Alps* a dozen times, the great majority of students would "own" that information. It became a part of them. Following completion of the day's work, there was another review. So lessons began and ended with review work. In math there was much drill work used in learning the multiplication tables. They had to be learned if any real progress in math was going to be made.

For those students who fell behind, I gave whatever extra help I could both during and after school. But looking back now on those early days of my teaching career, I can clearly see there was much for me to learn about remedial techniques and, most important, managing a classroom so I could have the maximum amount of time for students needing extra help. But Rome wasn't built in a day. (How's that for an original quotation?)

I may not have had much experience but the parents of my students seemed to be happy with their kids' progress. To show their appreciation and warmth, they invited me to dinner at their homes whenever I had to hang around until evening to attend PTA meetings, as well as on a number of Sundays. It was a long way to drive for Sunday dinner but there was no way I would have turned down such hospitality.

There was one parent, unfortunately, who was anything but happy with what was happening in my classroom. Notice I didn't refer to her as an "irate" parent. This term has been abused to death. If there were as many irate parents as indicated by the use of this term, teachers would need battle gear. I can't even count on the fingers of one hand the number of merely angry parents I've had to deal with, let alone the irate ones. Be that as it may, let's get back to the unhappy mom. Okay, it was about 3:15, I was beat, and just ready to start relaxing before picking up Jo at the dilapidated school where she taught.

Suddenly, into my classroom popped a woman I'll call Mrs. Steeplejack—unhappy and anxious to let both me and the whole world know it. I was told that because her daughter had an IQ of 150 (which was true), she should be getting special work to challenge her. That sounded perfectly logical to me. But a monologue went on for a considerable period of time. I couldn't seem to get a word in edgewise—most unusual for me! And so I became angrier and angrier. Now both of us were unhappy. Then, just like a Champagne bottle, I blew my top ... but good! Heaven only knows what I said, but I do remember a look of astonishment on Mrs. Steeplejack's face, a look that seemed to say, "Hey, you're just a public servant. I have the right to come here and display whatever attitude strikes my fancy and you are obliged to take it."

How sad the whole incident was. She was wrong in showing an abusive attitude, but with more maturity and restraint and a lesser amount of pride on my part, I might have ignored her abuse and pacified her. Something good might have come out of this unfortunate situation. But blowing my top ended the conference on a most dismal note. No constructive dialogue was possible after that.

That year at McKinley School was made difficult by a series of car problems that weren't resolved until April. What? With a new, gorgeous, impressive, stunning, prosperous-looking, midnight blue Jaguar, I could have possibly had car trouble? Listen, that Jag of mine had the same first, middle and last name: Trouble. I no sooner accepted delivery of the car than my troubles started in earnest. The gorgeous thing would not start. This superlative piece of machinery just sat there as the ignition button was pressed repeatedly. Not the slightest sound was to be heard. Upon investigation it was discovered that the battery was dead.

That problem was solved easily enough. But that wasn't the real source of the trouble. The battery was found to be in perfect condition. Yet, periodically, the car wouldn't start because the battery had gone dead.

The service department checked everything, especially the electrical system, and came up with nothing concrete. As a result, this hunk of midnight blue "gorgeosity" failed to take me to my destination on so many occasions that I began to dislike it with considerable intensity. I even resorted to name-calling: the Blue Pig, El Klunko, the Lovely Lemon, and other terms of "unendearment" were used when referring to this costly dud. Of course, every time my Lovely Lemon broke down it necessitated borrowing a car to get to school. The only alternative was commuting, which Jo and I had to resort to on one occasion due to my inability to find a car to borrow. What an awe-inspiring trip it was! I was so spent by the time I arrived at school that I hardly had the energy to take attendance. And to think that Jo had done this for years.

The kids and teachers were rather impressed with the collection of cars I seemed to have at my disposal. I assured them that I much preferred my Jag if only it would behave itself.

The low point was reached when I totally destroyed the transmission of a borrowed Cadillac. I'd been stuck in a snowbank near my house. In trying to get out of it, I stripped the gears in the transmission by changing too quickly from drive to reverse. Now I needed a substitute car for a substitute car. I was also in need of some money for a new transmission for the Cadillac!

Finally, after eight months of breakdowns and all their attendant headaches, I made up my mind to rid myself of this unending problem. I delivered the sick Jaguar to the dealer, deposited the keys on his desk, and notified him that the car and I no longer belonged to each other. Threatening to sue me, he became insistent that I keep the car. He was even willing to exchange the Jag for a new Oldsmobile convertible, in a deal involving no additional money. I'll admit I was tempted, but I resisted, figuring that any car that came from that dealer was apt to be bad news. No lawsuit followed, either.

In all fairness, when the Jag ran, its performance was marvelous. For some peculiar reason, however, even the Jaguar specialist I took it to couldn't keep it running properly. Strange how some cars have defects for which permanent remedies cannot be found. Such cars, in my opinion, should be officially designated "lemons," and their unlucky owners duly compensated by some governmental agency, just as crime victims are finally being awarded damages by some progressive states.

I lost a bundle on that Jaguar, so now my Champagne tastes could no longer be satisfied. My next car would have to be inexpensive and unpretentious. Within a day or so of parting with the Jag, I plunked down what in those days was the standard price for an older car—$100—and became the owner of a definitely unpretentious 1947 Ford convertible. Or was it a Mercury? I didn't have it long enough to really take notice. The next day I traded my newly acquired 1947 Whatever convertible for the best vehicle I've ever owned— a 1953 Plymouth convertible—a true jewel that ran even better than it looked. My car problems were solved at last. By some miracle I'd had the foresight to do this car-juggling act during my Easter vacation, which made matters much simpler.

The year had also been complicated by an unusual amount of snow, which I figured heralded the start of a new Ice Age. Oh, did it snow! One afternoon, despite blizzard-like conditions, a teachers' meeting was held after school. This was not a wise decision, for by the time the meeting was concluded, the roads were impassable. Jo and I were stranded. Luckily, we found refuge at a staff member's home.

Many times during our long rides, I'd mentioned to Jo how I planned to move to California for various reasons, most important of which was my desire to get away from snow and cold weather. Therefore, this was to be my one and only year at McKinley School. You can just imagine what Jo thought about having to go back to commuting. I'll tell you what she thought: No way ... I'm going to learn to drive.

In a matter of a week Jo had a car. Since her husband was also a nondriver, I taught her to drive. Once she'd learned, we drove to school much of the time with Jo proudly behind the wheel of her own car. Way to go, Jo!

As the year drew to a close I could look back with satisfaction on a year filled with novel experiences. Threatening for years to become airborne, I had finally taken the plunge and learned to fly. Even though I enjoyed teaching very much, I was still toying with the idea of a career in aviation. To everyone's advantage, the dream faded as I realized that with my laughable sense of direction I'd doubtless make Wrong Way Corrigan look like the paragon of navigational skills.

I flew over and around Westchester County Airport for about forty hours and then clipped my own wings. Before doing so I did have a rather memorable experience. One Friday I promised my sixth graders I was going to fly solo up the Hudson and pay them a little visit the next day. As I hopped into my rented Aeronca Champion and got ready for takeoff, I began wondering what kind of landing I'd be capable of making on the concrete runway to which I would be directed by the tower. My only experience in takeoffs and landings had been on the turf and I was well aware that there was a difference. I wasn't in the least bit worried about the takeoff. The landing was what had me somewhat concerned.

Although I'd heard it said dozens of times that any landing you can walk away from is a good one, I fervently hoped to do better than just that!

Off I went into a wild and not very blue yonder. First of all, Westchester County Airport, on that particular day, seemed to have every type of aircraft imaginable flying around it. It wouldn't have been surprising to have seen Lindbergh's *Spirit of St. Louis* flitting about somewhere within the environs. Second, the sky was hazy to an unprecedented degree. It reminded me of pictures I'd seen of smog in the Los Angeles area.

Feeling not very intrepid, I had taken to the air intent upon shooting at least one landing on the concrete runway before heading up the Hudson for my rendezvous with the kids. Not long after takeoff I realized that the haze was even worse than it had appeared from the ground. But first things first. I'd make one landing and then worry about the haze.

That first landing was a long time in coming. Aircraft were stacked up to such a degree that I had to circle the field repeatedly. The pattern was the same: head for the airport and be instructed by the tower to go around. This meant fly toward the Tappen Zee Bridge on the Hudson River; at that point make a 180-degree turn and head back for the airport. The sky was so crowded that day, that on one of my go-arounds I even discovered, just below my right wing, a flight of Air National Guard jet fighters following a jet which was towing a target.

With the completion of numerous go-arounds, I was, at last, cleared to land. This would be my first landing on a concrete runway. Hitting the runway like a rock, I bounced awkwardly, which caused me embarrassment. Meanwhile, the tower wanted to know whether I intended to land or simply touch and go around again. I decided to go around but almost stalled while making my intentions known to the control tower operator. At an altitude of fifty feet, a stall would have left both the aircraft and me badly in need of repair. And so began again the process of ring-around-the-airport. On my next opportunity to land, I made a good landing and called it a day. On Monday the kids were told just why their "daring" aviator-teacher was nowhere to be seen on Saturday.

I missed what must have been one of the most hilarious moments of the school year. During Christmas vacation I had taken a trip to Florida to visit a boyhood buddy. On my return I bought a baby alligator as a souvenir, something I felt my class would get a kick out of. I put it in a box and set the box next to me.

As I was driving along, I placed my hand on the box, not noticing in the darkness that it had come open slightly. One unhappy, little alligator responded by biting me. I had the feeling of being stuck with a bunch of fine needles. Letting out a screech, I decided the best place for this reptile would be in the car's trunk. I forgot, entirely, that alligators can't handle cold weather. By the time that 'gator was placed in the trunk it was unquestionably too cold for it to stay alive. And it didn't. When I opened the trunk on one of my stops, I saw one very dead baby alligator.

On my return to school, I brought the dead 'gator along. I wasn't happy about its condition but if I couldn't bring it back alive, dead was second best. One of my students suggested the little beast be taken to the principal's office for inspection—you know, kind of a practical joke. Two kids were entrusted with this task. When they returned, I asked them what her reaction had been. They indicated that she screamed and did other things characteristic of frightened people.

The school year had started off with my arriving at school in a very sedate Jaguar. By the time it concluded, I was pulling into the parking area with a red canoe slung securely onto the roof of my Plymouth convertible. For the life of me, I can't imagine why I hadn't removed it after a camping trip to the Adirondack Mountains.

Before the last day of school arrived, the kids knew I was California-bound. They gave me a list containing their addresses. I promised to send each of them a postcard from somewhere. I also received a living memento of McKinley School days. Linda Peterson gave me a part-husky puppy which I named Pilot. It would accompany me to California.

Chapter Three

Barry Had to Be Kidding

So you think California is so great! What about the smog and all that traffic? Don't you ever watch "Dragnet"? And the weird people! You think New York is strange? Wait until you see some of the kooks out in California!

This was the opinion, in capsule form, of a small group of friends and relatives. The majority, however, thought it could be a refreshing change. Smog and heavy traffic? There was no law compelling me to live where these conditions existed. For sure, I planned to give congested areas a wide berth. By "kooks" I assumed they were referring to persons who refused to live in a particular mold, who ardently believed in innovation. Hey, it might be nice to see a little variation from the Gray Flannel Suit Syndrome was my thought.

Admittedly, I was totally in love with California. Its names fascinated me: Santa Monica, Pacific Palisades, San Bernardino, Palm Springs, and most especially, Redondo Beach and Ventura. But, as I would discover later, none of these places were my speed, since they were situated in more or less heavily populated areas and I yearned for a rural setting—like those you see on California wine bottles.

37

Whatever plans I had for settling in California depended, of course, on my success in finding a teaching position. With some valuable experience to my credit, though, the job outlook appeared bright.

On a beautiful day in June, without much in the way of luggage, or for that matter, preparation, I hopped into my blue convertible and set out for California, where, according to one of my more sarcastic Bronx friends, the sun always shone and unhappiness in any form was unheard of.

Everything west of Ohio was new territory for me. With so much scenic beauty to look forward to, I fairly trembled with excitement. The great interstate highway system was still in its infancy but it was possible to travel from the New York Metropolitan Area to Chicago in thirteen hours via multi-laned toll roads through New Jersey, Pennsylvania, Ohio, and Indiana. You could get spoiled by that kind of driving. For once you left the Chicago area, it was back to the two-lane highways where driving could be frustrating *in extremis,* especially on winding roads. Anyone who has been forced to follow a four-wheeled "snail" for miles and miles will wholeheartedly agree with me.

Yet, driving cross-country on two-lane highways was interesting. It gave a person the opportunity, not only of getting a closer look at the country, but also of knowing something of its people and their customs in a way that isn't possible via today's superhighways. Nevertheless, for folks with time on their hands and romance in their souls, cross-country excursions on good, old fashioned, two-lane highways are still perfectly feasible.

Driving across the plains of Illinois, Iowa, and Nebraska was fascinating. I imagined the huge herds of buffalo that once roamed these seemingly endless stretches of grassland. It had taken an unbelievable amount of carnage to rid the plains of them. Fortunately, the killings were brought to an end before these magnificent beasts became extinct. Trainload upon trainload of their bones were eventually collected and converted into fertilizer.

Much of my driving was done at night. If I had restricted my driving to the daylight hours, I'd certainly have seen much more. But I enjoyed not only what I saw during the day but also what was to be seen at night. What could be more enchanting than a starlit night out in the middle of nowhere? I'll tell you what: a full moon rising over the mountains, bathing the entire countryside in its silvery light! How could I stop at a motel, conk out until morning, and deprive myself of such exquisite beauty?

Most of the time, as evening came, I would just keep on going. Such was my love of the open road and the lure of my destination—California. Whenever I was able to pick up a radio station with good music, so much the better. It was not without good reason that, years before, my Bronx buddies had bestowed on me the title Captain Midnight, a sort of Doctorate of Nocturnal Motoring! Even as a college kid I really dug those night shadows.

There were times, though, when Captain Midnight would have to pack it in for the night, but in diehard fashion, not usually earlier than one or two in the morning.

Upon arriving in Laramie, Wyoming, I decided to take a short detour through what promised, according to my map, to be spectacular mountain scenery. The Snowy Range in Medicine Bow National Forest could be seen off in the distance. Getting there required a long climb with many hairpin turns. On the way the road crossed a wide and beautiful plain where sheep were grazing. The sheepherder was nowhere to be seen but the presence of his wagon, with a thin plume of smoke rising lazily from the stovepipe, indicated he was on the job.

Reaching the foothills, I was much impressed with the surroundings: below, the lush valley dotted with sheep; above, the mountains in all their majesty. How would I handle the intoxicating beauty of a full moon in this setting? It was easy for me to see that this was only a prelude to one of the most breathtaking stretches of scenic beauty I was to see on my trip.

As the road climbed, little lakes and streams appeared, with fir trees resembling church spires scattered up and down the mountain slopes. Soon the snowline was reached. Now there were lakes containing ice, and large patches of snow everywhere. This amazed me. Imagine being able to make snowballs in June!

This setting contained so much that I considered precious, including solitude. Hardly another car was visible on that road. Walking over to a crystal-clear, icy brook lined with fir trees, I sat down and was serenaded by a choir of birds. There was an occasional solo and even a duet and trio thrown in for good measure. These birds must have sensed my awe and appreciation, for they produced encore after encore of the sweetest melodies. Heaven! This is what heaven must be like, I thought. Before leaving this Bambi-like dreamland I stopped again and again in an attempt to take in as much scenery as possible.

For any of my readers who may someday find themselves in the vicinity of Laramie, I'd highly recommend taking Route 130 through this pristine wonderland of mountain majesty. The highest point on this road is Snowy Range Pass. If you can take elevations of up to 10,800 feet, this trip to "Bambiland" is a must.

As I traveled through the desert, cruising along at sixty and seventy miles an hour on a smooth road with no angry and very determined Indians in hot pursuit, I couldn't help reflecting on the lot of those singularly rugged and gutsy individuals known as pioneers. How could such an inhospitable land be crossed? Its width was immense, drinkable water was practically nowhere to be found, the terrain was positively atrocious, and those terribly unhappy, war-whooping

Indians could appear at any time to provide havoc galore! And, as if these problems weren't sufficient, there was the tremendous heat to contend with, in addition to sickness and personality clashes. Is it any wonder that during one period of migration, graves averaged approximately one per mile? Yet, for the West to be settled, the pioneer was the breed of human being required, and the times produced just such a breed.

Arriving, at long last, in California, I noticed a transformation that was almost miraculous! Gone was the desert. In its place was a botanical wonderland, with mammoth trees, the likes of which I'd never seen before. And water ... blessed and beautiful water!

From a vista point high in the Sierra Nevada, Donner Lake appeared in all its sapphire splendor. The lake was named after an ill-fated party of Midwesterners who began their trek to California too late, considering they had to cross the high Sierra. By the time the party reached this lake, they found the going increasingly difficult as a result of the steady snowfall, one of the heaviest in California's history. Unable to travel any farther, they built log shelters and prepared to wait out the storms, but were marooned as the snow continued.

After six weeks, a party of ten men and five women set out on snowshoes to bring relief. A month later, under the harshest of conditions, seven survivors reached Sutter's Fort. They had been nourished en route by the bodies of the eight men who had died. A relief party was hurriedly sent back to the Donner camp, which had become a place of horror, where survival depended on cannibalism. When the rescuers reached the lakeside camp in February, 1847, the roughly built cabins were covered by thirteen feet of snow.

Of the eighty-two members of the Donner Party who had reached the Sierra, only forty-seven were to survive. Twenty-one perished in the death camp, thirteen on the trail over the summit, and one died in the Sacramento Valley.

In contrast, for me the Sierra's mountain greenery provided the perfect place for rest and relaxation; but I had important business ahead of me, namely, getting a job. And you know ... time and tide wait for no man! (How's that for another Sorgi original?) Coasting downhill seemingly all the way, I finally reached Roseville, in the Sacramento Valley, which was to be my first stop and kind of a home away from home. My mother had given me a letter of introduction to an old New York friend of hers living there. When I arrived at Grace Bernardini's house, her display of hospitality was both heartwarming and flattering. She didn't know what to do first for her good friend's son.

A few hours later, her husband, Mario, came home from work and the scene was more or less repeated. That was only the beginning. There were numerous relatives to whom I'd have to be introduced. If you know anything about Italian culture you can just imagine all the histrionics involved in these multiple introductions.

Oh, the food was so good ... and plentiful! ("Have you had enough to eat, Bob? Are you sure?") A cozy room was provided for me to rest my weary bones, after a grueling trip without the benefit of much rest.

Between the lush scenery, a general impression of the good life and insuperable hospitality, California was all I had hoped it would be. California, I thought, you're too beautiful to be true! Anyone living elsewhere is underprivileged.

There was no waste of time in looking for a teaching job. Because my teaching experience had been accepted in lieu of practice teaching, I was already licensed to teach in California. Now I had the confidence that comes with having all your papers in order. Surely getting a job would be a snap.

Leaving the home of those wonderful people, the Bernardinis, I headed for Northern California where the population was thinner and the spaces wider. Two hours later I figured I'd traveled far enough north and began looking for elementary schools. In the vicinity of Red Bluff I spotted one and stopped to inquire about possible teacher vacancies. The only person at the school was the *right* person, the Superintendent of Schools, Chuck Smith. He told me that, indeed, there was need of a teacher. Not in that particular school, but in the district's one-room school located in a logging camp, way out in the boonies.

Chuck took me outside to indicate just where this school was. He pointed a finger in the direction of a range of mountains. No doubt, it certainly was remotely situated! To get there required an hour's drive. Chuck didn't seem overly anxious to make the trip so I had to be satisfied with his description of the school and its surroundings. From the start, I was interested.

The salary was twenty percent more than what I'd made the previous year. Since peace, quiet, and mild winters were what I was looking for, with a chance to go fishing and traipsing around in the great outdoors, the position appeared to be fashioned just for me. With nothing negative to deter me, I decided to fill out the application form. Although Chuck didn't offer me a contract on the spot, there seemed little doubt that I'd get the job. Following an exchange of pleasantries and a handshake, I was off and running, headed back to New York to make preparations to move to California on a permanent basis.

I couldn't help wondering, though, what I'd do if I didn't get the job. The answer was quick in coming. I'd return to California anyway and resume my search! But why worry? was my thought. That teaching position was mine!

In a carefree, "what me worry?" mood, I decided to take a long detour through the Pacific Northwest and Canada.

The Oregon coast, with its steep cliffs, rugged evergreens, and colorful rhododendrons was stunning.

Even more stunning was the beauteous damsel dishing out ice cream in one of those Dairy Delight drive-ins. The degree of her comeliness was of such magnitude that I must have resembled a combination of the absent-minded professor and Mr. Magoo, as I mumbled and stumbled back to my car, ice cream in hand.

Besides an abundance of lovely forests, rivers, lakes, and snowcapped mountains, the state of Washington contains an area which can most aptly be described as lunar in appearance. Driving through the east-central part of the Evergreen State, I was struck by the bizarre topography and weird emptiness. It was nothing short of eerie! Fearful gusts of wind added to the spookiness of the scene. Just keeping my car on a steady course was a big chore, causing me a case of "heart-in-mouth" disease. Like ... get me out of here, and fast!

The next day, while going through Customs and Immigration in British Columbia, there occurred another of nature's angry displays, this time in the form of torrential rain. At least it wasn't frightening like the previous day's strange winds.

During that downpour there was nothing to do but relax and wait for it to let up. In the meantime, like a good little teacher, I kept my promise and wrote each of my former sixth graders a postcard. Writing twenty-eight of them caused me to strive for a little imagination since "Having fun, wish you were here" or one of its variations gets old fast.

Beautiful British Columbia. That's what it says on the province's license plates. If the plate were to be made bigger or the letters smaller, I'd suggest filling it with superlatives. In British Columbia I found myself making all kinds of silly sounds—"ooo," "ah," "eee"—as I gazed in complete astonishment at its endless wonders! Its neighbor, Alberta, isn't exactly lacking in "ooo's" and "ah's," either—not with such wonderlands as Banff and Jasper national parks.

Re-entering the United States at the Montana border, my reputation as Captain Midnight remained untarnished as I drove through the night with unflagging determination ... and with toothpicks keeping my eyelids from closing. So long, Montana! Hiya, North Dakota! See ya, North Dakota! Hello there, Minnesota!

At last, feeling like a ramblin' wreck, I simply had to terminate this thousand-mile marathon and pack it in at Bemidji, Minnesota. The motel I checked into was so new that my room had no draperies. This gave me the feeling of being on display. People whooping it up at a tavern close to the room added to my discomfort. After managing to slip into bed and undress under the covers while hoping that nobody would pass by, I was soon fast asleep.

Two days later I was back home, enumerating the advantages of California living to all who would listen—a sort of one-man California Chamber of Commerce. In short order the expected job offer arrived from California and I was again on the road. This time my baggage included Pilot, my dog. Because puppies will be puppies, he was to present me with a few problems I could very well have done without.

Any time I'd go to a restaurant, it was, of course, necessary to leave him in the car. On one occasion, the heat was so intense I decided to leave the car windows open. To prevent his jumping out, I snapped on his leash and secured it to the clutch pedal. As I was enjoying a snack, I heard a commotion outside the restaurant. What should I behold but Pilot hanging by his neck outside the car, notifying all within hearing range of his dire plight! After coming to his rescue, I informed him that he'd just totally ruined my lunch!

Three and three-quarter days after leaving The Bronx, I was back in California. My puppy's potty stops did cramp my style, but somehow his presence spurred me on.

My assignment was teaching a class of twenty kids in a nearly new, one-room school in a logging camp. The school was named after the tiny community: Lyman Springs. Its mountain setting could hardly have been more beautiful with tall, stately pines everywhere, a sky that was almost perpetually blue, and a peek at snow-covered Mt. Shasta off in the distance. But I did find two problems.

Problem number one was housing ... and it would have to be resolved quickly. School was to begin in just a few days. In the meantime I lived at the school: my bed, the schoolroom floor. Pilot would sack out close to me and snore the night away.

During the day I'd keep myself busy trying to solve problem number two: how in the world was it possible for one teacher to teach eight grades in one room? To be sure, there was at least one pupil enrolled in each of the eight grades, just to complicate matters. With no school telephone and the district office forty mountainous miles away, there was no doubt in my mind that I'd have to learn to be independent and wing it on many an occasion.

Not long after my arrival, I received the surprise of a lifetime. Told that there was a phone call for me at one of the private residences near the logging camp office, I wondered just who it could be. The "who" turned out to be Barry, a former student of mine from Marlborough Academy. He was calling from Toronto, Canada. We'd been corresponding since I left Marlborough fourteen months earlier, but how he'd ever sniffed me out here in these woodsy boonies, I never did find out.

The purpose of his call? He wanted to come stay with me and be in my class! After I patiently enumerated the 743 reasons why the possibility of this occurring was highly unlikely, Barry saw the light. Moreover, who had ever heard of a kid wanting to go from high school back to elementary school?

Just before the start of school, a cabin became available, solving my first problem. Sleeping in a bed was a pleasant change but using an outhouse was rather quaint, as was the absence of bathing facilities. But with luck on my side, it wasn't long before I was able to rent a cabin with all the amenities, even a television set. Things were looking better.

Yet, I was uneasy, aware that my second problem was still unsolved. I could not, no matter how hard I tried, figure out how I was going to teach all eight grades at the same time. Of little consolation was the knowledge that, at one time, the one-room school was the source of education for so much of America's population. It all boiled down to a crisis in self-confidence. I was accustomed to walking into a classroom and being in complete control, able to innovate on the spur of the moment. In this new situation, I hardly knew where to begin. The previous teacher, who had moved on to another one-room school nearby, gave me whatever pointers he could but I still didn't have a real handle on how to operate in a multigrade teaching situation.

The school day started with the raising of Old Glory and the California state flag. Following the Pledge of Allegiance, classwork began. The kids did their assigned work. Any of them needing help asked for it by raising a hand and, as quickly as possible, I'd be there to assist. Rest assured, I was always on the move, just like any teacher handling a multigrade teaching assignment.

A good deal of my time was devoted to teaching the first grade, consisting of three very cute little girls, all of whom were wanting their two front teeth for Christmas. To me, those kids were Obligation Number One since this was their first school experience and it was essential that they receive a solid foundation in the fundamentals. And what good learners they were! The three of them kept pace with one another in reading, writing, and arithmetic. They learned the alphabet and how to write legibly by printing five or six of the letters over and over each morning. I'd print the first of each day's letters, using a separate line for each letter. The kids would then have to complete each line, printing the letters slowly and carefully on specially lined primary school paper.

For math, they were expected to learn the simple addition and subtraction facts such as $3+4=7$, $8-6=2$ ... that sort of thing. This was accomplished by supplying them with a considerable number of examples wherein these facts were used repeatedly. Addition and subtraction flash cards came in handy, too. With access to countless pinecones, it's a pity that I never thought of using some as a means of making the learning of math facts more meaningful. (Here are five pinecones just for you, Genevieve ... Now, may I have two back, please? Thank you. How many do you have left, Genny? That's right. You've got three pinecones left. Wonderful!)

Every day, without fail, each of my toothless wonders read to me from the first grade reader. Their smooth, steady progress was gratifying. Also, without the necessity of remedial work, there was plenty of time to read them stories, providing me with the opportunity to ham it up. Concerning the first grade, then, I could say that I felt "right." My program was a success.

On the other hand, circulating around the room most of the day helping kids in the other grades who were stumped on work, which they were trying to teach themselves, was frustrating. It caused me to feel inadequate to the task, as if something weren't being done right. There had to be a more efficient way to teach in a multigrade situation.

Unfortunately for the kids in grades two through eight, and also for me, I never really got my act together. Oh, things looked fine outwardly. The class was conducted in an orderly manner, even though I generally didn't know whether I was coming or going. There were no petitions to have me "deported" back to The Bronx. I got along well with the kids, although one confirmed maverick caused me occasional pain throughout several parts of my anatomy. There were dinner invitations that I most hastily and gratefully accepted because any talent that I may have had in the art of cooking was yet to be discovered. And after many visits even the superintendent had nothing negative to say. Yet, I was anything but happy with my work and counted the days until this frustrating assignment would come to a conclusion.

My contract included janitorial duties. At the close of each day, one of the older kids would volunteer to help me. As a result, the clean-up was completed quickly, enabling me to get away from school a bit earlier than expected, and try to forget that teaching, the joy of my life, had lost some of its glow. My favorite method of forgetting was to go fishing in any of a number of crystal-clear creeks not far from home. I never met with much success but it was relaxing for both Pilot and me.

That dog of mine wanted to be everywhere I was ... even in the classroom. Wouldn't he have looked cute in school "helping" me bumble my way through another day? Each morning Pilot would try his best to follow me to school as I drove there in my car. This displeased me greatly. The issue could have been settled easily enough by tying him to a tree near the house. But it would have been an extremely noisy proposition with a most unhappy dog "serenading" the neighbors and making them miserable, perhaps even angry.

What to do to cause the least misery to all parties concerned? Well, each morning I'd rev up the engine of my car and make a mad dash down the narrow, dusty, winding road lined with trees, and literally outrace my overly enthusiastic dog to the point where his endurance gave out and he'd quit running. Pilot would trot back home to patiently (or impatiently) await my return seven hours later. This scene was repeated every single morning. Miraculously, both the car and I survived without a scratch!

It was at Lyman Springs School that I first came into contact with Indians. There were five of them in my class— all from the same family—and I was thrilled silly to be their teacher, for studying Indians of the Americas was a hobby of mine. I could have learned quite a bit about old Indian ways from this pleasant family from Nevada, but somehow never got around to doing much delving.

For one so interested in Indians, the real pity was that I did no research on tribes that had inhabited the area in which I lived and taught. By doing so I would have learned of Ishi, the Yahi Indian, who, as the sole survivor of his tribe, stepped out of the wilds of Tehama County in 1911 to enter a civilization totally foreign to him.

He was referred to as the last wild Indian of North America, and placed by the federal government under the care of the Department of Anthropology of the University of California. Ishi, the man who emerged from the stone age, spent the remaining five years of his life among people who treated him with great kindness and admiration.

Regardless of my having no yen for one-room schoolhouse teaching, California remained tops in my book. It was *the* place to live. As time went by, I tried to convince my parents, my sister and brother and their spouses, along with my Aunt Mary, to move to California. The approach used was probably similar to that used by other former New Yorkers trying to get their families and friends out to the West Coast. My pitch went something like this: Every day since I've been here the sky's been blue and the temperature just perfect. I'll bet it's hailing, sleeting, and snowing in New York as you're reading this letter. Wouldn't it be sweet to get away from driving in all that dirty, slippery, dangerous snow? And how about the subway? Can you imagine how great it would be to take your last ride in a packed subway train, knowing that you'd never again have to feel like a sardine?

The sales pitch I used on my brother, an upstate New York dairy farmer, was also anything but original: John you've got to be kidding, farming in a place where you've got to mess with oodles of snow, plus thirty-below! Come to California where the grass isn't only greener, but grows all year long!

At the conclusion of my one-room schoolhouse teaching stint I headed back to New York with my dog. Leaving my car at a friend's ranch, Pilot and I flew home to New York.

Of course, my propaganda campaign intensified and ultimately proved highly successful. Only my brother and his family stayed in the East. My parents and I settled in Santa Cruz, on California's beautiful central coast. The rest of the family made their homes in San Jose and San Francisco.

There was no way of knowing it at the time, but all sorts of nice things were headed my way!

Chapter Four

Professor Sorgionoff

"Bob, what do you know about team teaching?" Eminently qualified to make such an inquiry was the Superintendent of Schools of Freedom, California, Dr. Andrew Adams—better known as just plain Andy—a man big on innovations (If it's new, it *must* be good!).

Andy was big in another respect ... size. As he sat in his wheelchair puffing away on a pipe, I couldn't help wondering just how tall he would be if he stood up to his full height.

Intelligently answering his question about team teaching was complicated by an office filled with sports pictures, trophies, plaques, and athletic equipment to which my eyes had become riveted. The man in the wheelchair obviously had quite a sports background. I was certainly more interested in interviewing Andy Adams than I was in being interviewed by him!

Upon informing the superintendent that team teaching was just what it sounded like—classes being taught by a team of teachers—we got down to discussing the "real important stuff": baseball. And did we talk!

Andy never mentioned what had put him in a wheelchair for life, but he did tell me about his baseball career in general and, most interestingly, the tryout he'd had with the Cleveland Indians. He then pointed himself out in a small group picture of Cleveland players all suited up in their home uniforms. He looked positively great, like a ballplayer's ballplayer: tall, handsome, athletic—youth at its finest. Seeing him sitting in a wheelchair presented quite a sad contrast, especially since he was still so young.

In the midst of our baseball discussion, Andy interrupted himself to call in his principal. As clear as a bell I can still hear him calling, "Duane." That's all he said. In a matter of seconds Duane Crawford stepped into the office. Following a hasty introduction, Andy told me that Duane had also played professional baseball ... with Portland of the Pacific Coast League, just one step below the New York Yankees. And for my further information, Owen Hand, one of his sixth grade teachers, had played semipro ball with a number of players who were now in the major leagues.

While so much baseball was being discussed, I can remember thinking: If there must be such things as interviews, let them all be like this—talking baseball. Little did I know what was coming up eventually.

Andy suggested that I go into the teachers' lounge and relax, which I gladly did, stretching out and actually catching a little shut-eye. (I can't imagine being quite that casual, but one teacher who claimed to see me snoozing assured me over the years that, yes, I sure did nap contentedly.)

At the completion of my rest period, at which point it was lunchtime, the interview was resumed in this highly improbable fashion: Andy put on his baseball cap, wheeled himself out to the closest baseball field and planted himself firmly on the pitcher's mound. Duane took his position at first base, I covered third base, while six junior high kids were chosen for the remaining positions. A game against a very competent junior high team then got under way. Mind you, I was dressed to impress: tie, blazer, dress slacks, good shoes, the works. Andy and Duane were also attired in other than casual sportswear. (I kept thinking, This is some interview!)

I haven't the faintest idea of how long the game lasted, who won, or, for that matter, whether or not I ate. But after the game the interview continued in Andy's office. Something having to do with teaching must have been discussed ... probably how to figure out a baseball player's batting average! It's hard to imagine a longer, more segmented "interview." At its conclusion, Andy took a piece of paper, which looked as if it had been through the mill, smoothed it out and wrote, in simplest form, using a pencil, an agreement to hire me. Thus began eight of the most fruitful and enjoyable years of my life!

Freedom is a small, basically agricultural community adjoining Watsonville. The area's agriculture includes apples, strawberries, lettuce, and various other garden vegetables. At one time it was known as Whiskey Hill. Heaven knows what kind of unsavory activities were commonplace in town during those early years, what with such a name!

Freedom School, when I started teaching there, consisted of about a dozen gray, wooden buildings which had been part of a U.S. naval air station during World War II. The old administration building containing the school office still had a ship's bell mounted near the door. Directly across the street from the school office was the sixth grade building comprising four classrooms, a teachers' lounge, and living quarters for the head custodian. The setup was wonderful, especially the lounge part, which provided the four sixth grade teachers with a quiet place to work or just relax during breaks.

Of course, there was always the main lounge where teachers went for diversion of one sort or another. For the most part, the main lounge was a pretty fun place with much laughter. It could become a bit hairy, though, as on one occasion I remember so well.

One of the married male teachers evidently had been spreading the word that an unmarried female staff member was hopelessly in love with him. Well, said woman got wind of this and suddenly, in the normally fun-filled or at least peaceful lounge, gave vent to her wrath in these angry and most unexpected words: "How dare you go telling everyone that I'm in love with you!" Other equally stunning words followed, very, very few of them being spoken by the thoroughly embarrassed guy who appeared to be trying to vanish into the woodwork in an attempt to escape from this eruption of feminine fury.

Naturally, all other activity came to an immediate standstill. The noncombatants were in the middle of a private soap opera production and were most attentive as to what the next scene might be. This surprising scenario was of short duration but, search as I may, it has always remained tops in my memory of teachers' lounge drama.

Back to the sixth grade building. I shouldn't have even been there. My assignment had been a fourth grade team teaching deal. But without so much as a word from the administration regarding a change in teaching position, I found myself assigned to teach a sixth grade class, which suited me just as well. The team teaching plans disappeared without a trace, causing me to shed not even one tear, since I was anxious to get back to regular classroom teaching after all the frustrations of the Lyman Springs experience.

Each class seems to have a character all its own, a composite of the various personality types found within the group. That first crew of mine at Freedom School was totally unforgettable, as unique a group as I've ever encountered. The girls, all of them, were beautifully behaved. If that class had been made up solely of them, there would have existed the perfect class. But there supposedly is no such thing, and that year my class included a number of boys who more than guaranteed that the idea of the perfect class was merely a myth.

I was accustomed to running a tight but happy classroom and intended doing the same with this class. However, before a happy atmosphere could be created, the group of boys I'll refer to as the "feisty few" had to be tamed, because they had a rare genius for causing mayhem. In order to accomplish this task, records were set for the number of "punish lessons" dished out.

As a rule, if I needed to punish a kid, it was done by having him write each word in a spelling chapter a certain number of times, depending on the seriousness of the offense. Each chapter contained twenty-four words. Let's say a student made a habit of coming to class late, with no legitimate excuse. In that case he might have to write each of the twenty-four words twenty or twenty-five times. This little five-finger exercise was usually nasty enough to cause the tardiness to be cured immediately. If this simple remedy didn't work or the assignment wasn't completed, the little five-finger exercise became a big five-finger exercise. Each word would have to be written forty or fifty times. There was no way of getting out of it. The assignment had to be on my desk at the beginning of the next school day. Excuses, like My dog ate some of the pages, or My cat went potty on my punish lesson, were dismissed as being quite imaginative, but really!!

The most common excuse was: I did it, Mr. Sorgi, but left it at home. In most cases I'd tell the student I believed his story but the assignment included not only the writing part but also its being handed in to me at school. Therefore, the assignment had to be done a second time with both of them due on my desk first thing in the morning. It really hurt me to do this, especially when I was certain that the punish lesson had been completed. This was a tough policy but I felt it taught the kids much in the way of responsibility.

It also gave them a taste of the real world they would be entering in the not too distant future, where excuses such as I wasn't in court because I forgot all about my speeding violation, would be totally unacceptable.

That one-of-a-kind class had its problems primarily during recesses and lunch breaks, at which time arguments and fights would occasionally be started by the "feisty few." Whenever I was on yard duty and noticed any trouble brewing, I'd try to get things squared away quickly. One method of breaking up fights and getting the combatants to even laugh at the whole thing was for me to, first of all, stop the fists from flying by breaking up the fracas. Then I would assume the role of a boxing referee and, with a gravelly voice, announce: "In this corner wearing chartreuse trunks with pink, black and blue polka dots and weighing 250 pounds, we have Joey Beautiful, looking just gorgeous. And in the opposite corner, wearing orange trunks with seventeen black stripes and weighing in at 270 pounds, is Tiger Terrible, looking terrific."

At this point everybody would be laughing, including the former "mortal" enemies, and the problem would be quickly resolved. I used this procedure not only with my own kids but also with any students involved in fights.

During those times when I wasn't on yard duty and somebody in my class got into trouble, many a volunteer was more than willing to give me a blow-by-blow account of the whole mess even before getting into the classroom. Once in class, I would attempt to get the facts straight, an awesome task with a whole bunch of kids just dying to tell me what had happened. There'd be so many different versions as to what took place on the playground that it would cause me to wonder whether we were all discussing the same incident.

On one occasion, virtually the whole class got carried away with itself and went a bit bananas. (Maybe it was on one of those windy days when kids tend to become super-hyper.) Anyway, a whole bunch of my kids were chasing one another around my almost new Volkswagen convertible and acting pretty dopey, in general. They shouldn't have been in the parking area to begin with. From the main teachers' lounge—where periodically, soap operas were produced—I noticed that suddenly the racing and chasing stopped. The kids started examining one of my car's headlights. I went out to "help" them examine it.

Well, they'd succeeded in pushing in the headlight. I was most unhappy at their behavior in general, and my messed up headlight in particular! Although feeling very grumpy, I kept my mouth totally shut. By hand, I signaled for the class to line up and enter the classroom. Without uttering so much as a grunt, I wrote on the blackboard precisely what I wanted them to do. The whole class was to spend the afternoon writing lines, probably something like, We must not destroy our teacher's car. At the end of the afternoon they were dismissed without a word. Oh, how I wince now when I think of those few kids who spent an afternoon writing lines, yet had nothing whatsoever to do with the incident!

Within the confines of the classroom, disciplinary problems were almost nonexistent. My twenty-nine sixth graders were trustworthy enough for me to be able to take an occasional short break in the small lounge just down the hall from the classroom. After leaving the room, I'd pause a moment or two before heading for the lounge, just to make sure that my leaving didn't precipitate World War III. It never did. Those kids were positively angelic, working quietly on a written assignment, usually spelling.

To be sure, I exercised enough caution to avoid pushing my luck. More than ten minutes away from my class might have been asking for little incidents to start taking place. Consequently, I limited myself to a quick cigarette and then returned to the classroom to find everything in perfect order. As the year progressed, I no longer felt it necessary to pause near the door after leaving the room, feeling that the kids had earned my trust.

It was so strange that the "feisty few" were able to exercise self-control in an unsupervised classroom, yet were capable of total barbarism in the play area, which was supervised! (This foolish practice of leaving children in a classroom unattended has long since been abandoned.)

A couple of years after leaving sixth grade, the feistiest member of the notorious "feisty few" dropped into my room for a visit. I was in the midst of counseling a student on ways and means of avoiding warlike behavior. Seeing that I was busy, my former "problem number one" left the room, but not before informing the boy being counseled that I was "as fair a teacher as you could find." Yes indeed, the feistiest of them all had mellowed and matured, thank goodness!

The subject we spent the most time on was social studies. I can still remember the name of the textbook we used. It was entitled *Our American Neighbors,* and was devoted chiefly to a study of the geography and history of Latin America. The subject matter was presented in such an interesting way that it made teaching it a joy.

What we all found fascinating and incredible was that the Spanish Conquistadors were able to conquer the well-organized Aztecs of Mexico and Incas of South America, both numbering in the millions, with a mere handful of soldiers totaling, in each case, about three hundred.

One reason this was possible was because the Spaniards possessed horses, firearms, and suits of armor, all unknown to the astonished Indians, who, at first, believed that the horse and its rider were one creature. Imagine their surprise when they observed horses and riders parting company!

Just a few of the other topics which generated special interest included the island of Saba, the Atacama Desert, the "chocolate-covered" streets of Guayaquil, Ecuador, the llama and, of course, the Christ of the Andes statue.

The West Indian island of Saba actually has a town built at the bottom of an extinct volcano. The town's name is, appropriately, Bottom.

Ask people, at random, to name the driest desert in the world. If they come up with a name, almost invariably the answer will be The Sahara, what else? Nope. The correct answer is the Atacama Desert of northern Chile, where in certain areas, it hasn't rained for hundreds of years.

The "chocolate-covered" streets of Guayaquil, Ecuador, are not really covered with chocolate. In truth, all they're covered with is a layer of cacao beans from which chocolate is made. The beans are set out to dry in streets around the processing plants where eventually they're made into chocolate.

One of the most useful animals in the world is the llama, whose home is in the Andean highlands of South America. This member of the camel family not only carries its master's burdens and provides wool for clothing but is also a source of food, and its dung is used for fuel. But try to force a llama to do something against its will and you may get a face full of spit!

Warmaking seems to stir the collective imagination of combatants to unheard-of heights. For example, during one South American battle, cheeses were actually fired from cannons when cannonballs were no longer available. True, cheeses are infinitely softer than your average cannonball. But how would *you* like to get belted with a big chunk of cheese shot from a cannon?

Unfortunately, when it comes to peacekeeping, the human race has only rarely shown much ingenuity. One of the most heart-warming stories in the human experience, however, took place in South America early in the present century.

War between Chile and Argentina seemed inevitable because of a border dispute. Wisely, the two nations agreed to divide the disputed mountain land, thus avoiding bloodshed. To remind themselves that peace is better than war, both countries decided to melt their cannons to make a statue of Christ. Mules then dragged the statue partway up steep mountain trails. Eventually, many soldiers and sailors from these two South American nations hitched themselves to ropes and hauled the statue up to Uspallata Pass, on the border of Argentina and Chile. Today the statue, called the Christ of the Andes, stands 12,000 feet above sea level. At its base is an inscription that reads: Sooner shall these mountains crumble into dust than Argentines and Chileans break the peace sworn at the feet of Christ the Redeemer.

To make learning and retaining the large volume of social studies facts easier, I would write a summary of each chapter at its conclusion, make copies of it, and distribute these copies to the kids. By the end of the year, each student had a complete summary of the subject matter which had been covered.

Question-and-answer periods were always exciting, as many students would have a hand raised in response to questions asked. The room could become a bit noisy as each student with a raised hand implored me to allow him to answer the question by calling my name frantically: "Mr. Sorgi! Mr. Sorgi! Mr. Sorgi!" (I'd refer to this in later years as being Sorgiized.) But the noise didn't bother me. It was a "good sound" since it was a result of being excited about learning.

And that's exactly what my goal was and still is—to get kids all fired up about learning; to motivate them to a degree wherein learning becomes a vital and thrilling part of their lives. How great to have children come up to my desk with loads of extra information on the subject matter being studied. Makes me feel like a millionaire!

For science, the class had another teacher, Professor Sorgionoff. This guy looked like me, was the same age, had a name half of which was identical to mine, spoke with a Russian accent and claimed Bulgaria as his native land. He would walk into the room, very business-like, each time informing the students that his name was Professor Sorgionoff from Bulgaria—as if the kids were likely to forget. Through the use of a science kit which was kept in the classroom, the professor would then perform an experiment, meanwhile chattering away with his heavy but quite understandable Russian accent.

Of greatest interest to the class was the distillation of water, since water that started out in one container at the beginning of the demonstration wound up in another one at the conclusion of it, with neither container having been moved or even touched. Without fail, whenever Sorgionoff entered the room, the kids would laugh. Was I embarrassed at this apparent show of disrespect? Certainly not! I loved the laughter immensely, because "Professor Sorgionoff" was really none other than Mr. Sorgi!

I've expressed my belief that discipline is the "big D," without which both teacher and class suffer: the teacher neurologically, the class academically. While the "big D" sets up the basic environment necessary for learning, the "big L," laughter, helps ease tensions which develop in any classroom.

One morning in that exciting first year at Freedom School, I discovered, strictly by accident, a way of getting laughs out of notes that kids brought from home. This particular note was an excuse for a boy's absence. Well, after Richard handed me the note and I'd read it, I decided to change its contents rather drastically. The note stated that he had been absent for some perfectly common reason like having a cold. Without even looking up from my desk I began reading in a serious voice easily heard by the entire class:

Dear Mr. Sorgi,

Please excuse Richard for being absent yesterday. The poor kid finds your class awfully boring and terrible beyond belief! As a matter of fact, I agree with him—your teaching is strictly for the birds and I wouldn't blame Richard if he played hooky everyday.

Sincerely,
Mary Zwicker

In the meantime, it took poor Richard a few seconds to catch on that it was a big gag and he nearly died of embarrassment. But the kid quickly joined with the rest of us in starting the day off with a hearty laugh.

Later that day he told his parents about the joke and they got in on it, too. Sure enough, next time Richard had to bring a note from home, he brought two of them, both signed by his parents. As I started reading the first note silently, it took me no time to realize that it was a gag. Immediately I began reading it aloud for the whole class to hear. There was lots of laughter, as the note described in detail what a rotten teacher I was and how much Richard dreaded coming to school. When I told the kids that the boy's parents had actually written the note, they really cracked up! Meanwhile, the class saw Richard standing by my desk, grinning from ear to ear as he handed me the real note.

Years later, one of those gag notes backfired, causing me much momentary embarrassment. Kathy, a fourth grader, brought an absence note up to my desk. Deciding that we could use a joke, and without paying the least bit of attention to what was written in the note, I started reciting the contents of a make believe note:

Dear Mr. Sorgi,
Please excuse Kathy's absence. I kept her home
so that we could play Monopoly.

P.S. She won.

Yours truly,
Mrs. Monahan

The kids got a big kick out of this zaniness. So did I, until
I read the note—which stated that Kathy was absent because of her grandfather's death! Following many apologies,
I made up my mind that, henceforth, whenever the yen possessed me to goof off with notes, I'd read them first!

The nicest thing that happened to me that year, or, for
that matter, any year, was meeting Sue. Her first glimpse
of me was of a guy wearing a bright red sweater and holding
a large bottle of red wine. The occasion was an evening fish
fry.

Earlier that day I'd gone deep-sea fishing out of Monterey
with a group of friends. They caught plenty of fish but my
chief occupation was coping with seasickness! By the time
we got back to the dock, I'd had more than my fill of deep-
sea fishing.

One of the girls in the group then suggested that we have
a fish fry at her home. My stomach felt as empty as a vac-
uum, so the idea was most appealing. Letting it be known
that my fish-cleaning skills were of championship caliber, I
was put to work cleaning fish, all the while anticipating a
solid meal. But it wasn't meant to be.

Now I'm well aware that garlic is considered indispens-
able in the art of cooking. I've also been informed countless
times that for a person of Sicilian ancestry to hate garlic
is tantamount to cultural treason. Be that as it may ... I
absolutely hate garlic!! Even arsenic sounds more appetiz-
ing! So what did one of the guys do but load all the fish

and bread with garlic! It was no practical joke, either. He just wasn't aware that not everyone can handle the stuff. Naturally, I was so repelled by the aroma that I opted for the only remaining source of nourishment, the wine that Sue saw me about to drink when she arrived at the fish fry with a group of her friends.

Eventually we all ended up at a beach in nearby Pacific Grove. Sue and I barely spoke to each other at the beach. I even went home early. So from all appearances, the day had been a disaster.

A few days later, though, I met Sue again at a gathering of friends and that did it ... but good! In less than two months we were engaged. Our first date was something along the lines of a Fred MacMurray–Claudette Colbert comedy of the '40s. The day was September 1st, just three days away from my first teaching day at Freedom and my initial encounter with the "feisty few."

I arrived at her home in Salinas on time and all spiffed up. Sue sure made the dress she was wearing look gorgeous! I was introduced to her parents, Al and Iva Rianda, and we all sat around making small talk for a few fidgety minutes— all, that is, except her father, who had his nose more or less buried in a newspaper. Then we were off to Monterey where we spent most of the evening at an elegant nightclub. We did a lot of dancing and I sang as we danced. The courtship might have ended right there on the dance floor, as Sue, using the type of diplomacy known to start wars, bluntly hinted that she'd heard foghorns with approximately the same tone! This revelation came as a complete shock since I was accustomed to girls complimenting me on my singing voice. Nevertheless, the evening was salvaged as I kept my mouth shut while dancing and simply let my feet do the talking.

Before taking Sue home, we went for a drive to Pacific Grove. I had every intention of getting my lovely date home at a respectable hour but a situation developed that made that impossible.

As we were driving near Pacific Grove, we noticed a young, well-dressed couple standing by the roadside, hitchhiking. The man looked a little worse for the wear. Sue and I decided we should stop. They were hitchhiking because the guy, a Navy pilot, had just driven his Volkswagen Bug over a steep embankment, changing the car's shape appreciably. His own shape could have been better, and there were indications that prior to the accident he would have had an "interesting," if not impossible time trying to thread a needle.

He asked that he and his girlfriend be taken to his home in nearby Pebble Beach. Just as we got there, the fellow noticed that his wallet containing much cash was missing. Back we drove to the wreck in search of it. Somehow we managed to find the wallet quickly. Back to his home we went.

By this time a "respectable" hour for getting Sue home had long since come and gone. The guy was superfriendly and in no rush to see us leave. He asked us to stay until dawn and have breakfast. At this point Sue called her parents and explained the unique situation and got permission to stay. Was I happy!

We danced until dawn and breakfasted with people who'd been total strangers just a few hours before. By the time I got Sue home at the insane hour of 7:00 A.M., it felt as though we'd been on two dates.

One result of meeting Sue was the realization that it would be a good idea to be more conservative with money. How else could I save enough money for an engagement ring and our marriage, which was eventually planned for the following June 9th?

Before long, I was moonlighting as an insurance salesman, calling at the homes of prospects by appointment only.

The appointments were obtained by a gal who went through the Watsonville phone book so many times she almost had it memorized. As a salesman, I quickly learned to expect the unexpected.

On one memorable call, the situation that developed was so strange I could hardly believe it was happening. Because the house was way out in the country and the road leading to it was flooded, just getting to the place was an adventure. With me that evening was a new salesman whom I was training. We arrived at the appointed time and were admitted into the farmhouse by an older couple. There were the usual introductions and small talk. Everything appeared to be perfectly normal.

No sooner had the talk turned to insurance than the woman got up from her seat, picked up a newspaper, and started swatting at objects—chairs, the table, the walls—at the same time saying, again and again: "I'm going to join the John Birch Society, that's what I'm going to do!" The trainee and I were flabbergasted, and even more so when the disturbed woman began drifting from room to room, turning the lights off and on, off and on. Let's face it, making sales with the lights on in peaceful surroundings can be difficult enough. With one of your prospects roaming around the house playing with the lights, swatting at objects with a newspaper, and talking incoherently, the task becomes definitely formidable. Her poor husband, who understandably became very distracted by the commotion, kept apologizing for his wife's bizarre behavior, while gently pleading with her to calm down.

Under these circumstances, my cohort and I, as quickly and smoothly as possible, said our good-byes and eased ourselves out of the house. On our way to the next appointment, we had plenty to say to each other about what we'd just witnessed.

It wasn't long before I became thick-skinned and able to face tense situations without squirming too much. But I never did run into anything even remotely approaching the scene we observed that evening.

Each year in March, the sixth graders at Freedom School used to spend a week at a nature camp in the midst of a redwood forest, along with other sixth graders from the area. The teachers went along, too, but their duties were minimal because the camp counselors took over almost completely. The hitch was that teachers were obliged to be at the camp from the time their classes arrived on Monday morning until they left on Friday afternoon. There was no going home, and you had to be available from 7:00 A.M. to approximately 10:00 P.M., with very little to do but just be "available"!

The idea was wonderful and gave kids a chance to learn much about the great outdoors. But now that I was engaged and holding down a second job, being enthusiastic wasn't easy. After all, I wouldn't be able to see Sue, nor earn any extra money selling insurance.

What a week it was! First of all, it rained and rained. I no longer wondered why the redwood trees grew so big. With all that rain they should have been as tall as Jack's beanstalk! Actually, I like rain because it can be beautiful and a treat to the senses, whether in the country or city. Rain and children, however, don't really mix that well, especially in a setting where there are many puddles. Invariably, children gravitate toward them, getting themselves soaked and causing needless complications. But that week, with hikes taking place rain or no rain, day and night, the kids were wet much of the time anyway. So the puddles hardly mattered.

Having to be available, I went along and suffered, not because of the rain or the risk of breaking bones while stumbling around in the dark, but because the big toe of my right foot was badly infected. It got so bad that I asked to be excused from some of the activities, particularly those faintly resembling commando training. It was a week to remember, all right! By its conclusion on Friday, I was glad to get home and relax following those fifteen-hour days.

The school year was drawing to a close, and fast. It had been a very rewarding year, but with my wedding day and the start of a seven-week honeymoon planned for the day after school closed, I was eagerly looking forward to the last day of school.

My class had long since been introduced to Sue. They "dug her the most," as has been the case with people who've met my wife and best friend during the past twenty-four years. Sue claimed that some of the girls' noses were out of joint when she showed up at school, but that didn't stop them from liking her.

One fine day she gave the class quite a surprise. Races had been held at the school to determine the champion runners, both boys and girls. At their conclusion, it was decided that the speediest girl in my class should race Sue. I can still see Sue and Linda racing at breakneck speed. My bride-to-be outdistanced the young speed merchant, but not by very much. I don't think any of the kids expected Linda to lose to an adult, a lady who was getting married, yet. The day of the woman athlete was still in the future.

Several years later, I tried the same thing with my fastest sixth grader, beating him by the hair on my chinny-chin-chin ... and then requiring two hours to catch my breath!

Many people in love write love letters. (Isn't that a brilliant conclusion?) I was one of the many ... and loved writing them. The stationery I sometimes chose wasn't what you'd normally expect love letters, or any other kind of letters, to be written on, but paper is paper.

I used to collect huge quantities of the children's crayon drawings. Some of this artwork was so cute that I'd ask the kids responsible for producing it for permission to keep it.

Not only was it flattering to the kids, it also gave me a most original form of stationery.

During music class, at which time the music teacher instructed my students in the art of singing, I would head for the sixth grade lounge and write Sue a love letter on the back of one of these crayon drawings. Wow, did I feel clever!

While on the subject of love letters, years after we were married, Sue and I dug out the love letters that we'd written to each other. As we read them, we squirmed and probably even blushed. That's how corny they sounded! When we got the nerve to read some of them to our children, they immediately experienced fits of uncontrollable and prolonged laughter. Such is love! It can cause people to write unbelievably silly things that, at the time they were written, sounded "supercool" or its equivalent.

Besides love letters, other things originated at Freedom School. One evening at an open house, a group of kids pleaded with me to adopt two homeless and very tiny kittens. One was a tabby, the other all gray. There wasn't a chance of refusing their request after the kids said the mother cat had been killed.

I thought of the perfect home for them. How could Sue or her parents refuse such pitiful, mewing, little bundles of fur? Unexpectedly, I dropped in on Sue after open house, with a kitten in each hand. No sales talk was needed. Those kittens now had an official address. Because they'd been fed solely by their mother and she was dead, the major problem was feeding them. Sue's father, who had a soft spot for cats, quickly found a doll's baby bottle. The kittens fed from it as if it were their own mother.

But there was one complication connected with their feeding. In the middle of the night, the two tiny felines would scream and holler to be fed. Like a perfect substitute for the mother cat, and despite the fact that it may have been two or three o'clock in the morning, Sue bottle-fed them with, I'm sure, a beatific smile on her amiable countenance.

When it came to naming the kittens, we must all have been lacking in imagination, for the best we could do in the way of names was Lightness for the tabby kitten and Darkness for the gray one. They found a most comfortable abode at Sue's place and lived there happily for many years. From cat heaven, wherever that might be, we're certain that Lightness and Darkness are forever throwing us kisses in gratitude for all the tender loving care we provided.

The last day of school, June 8th, arrived. Anyone who knows anything about the last day of school anywhere, knows that on this day children are hyper, some to the degree that if they were to lift their arms and flap them a bit, flight would become a distinct possibility! So what did I do to try to get through that last day of school without permanent psychological scars? Simply this: I had the kids write *very* lengthy compositions describing their year in my class. This was not only time consuming but also quite revealing. It afforded me the opportunity to find out what the kids thought of the way our class had been run, a kind of report card for me. To my delight, my students considered me strict but fair ... with more than just a tendency to act like a clown.

On completion of this assignment, we went outside and the kids had "free play" for the remainder of the day. In other words, they did whatever struck their fancy, as long as it stayed within the bounds of civilized behavior. I played catch with a few of the kids for a while, then chose to just relax and do nothing but observe.

At long last, dismissal time came, and my unique crew of twenty-nine received their report cards, officially making them seventh graders; and with expressions such as Have a nice summer, See you in September, and Happy Wedding Day ringing in my ears, the kids left for a well-earned summer vacation ... and I, with a sigh of relief, headed home, looking forward to my wedding the very next day.

Chapter Five

Symphony on a Theme by Volks

"Just think, Robert, some people go through this wedding day pandemonium many times," my sister commented, as she laughed her head off watching me racing around the house like a madman. She, her husband and four young children had just come from San Jose. Their arrival had been anxiously awaited, being that they were delivering my tuxedo, without which I could go nowhere.

The clock told me, in no uncertain terms, that the thirty-eight mile trip from Santa Cruz to the church in Salinas had better be getting started if we were to be there by the time the wedding was scheduled to begin, at eleven o'clock. So off we went, my sister and her family in their Cadillac, and my parents, Aunt Mary, and me in my beautiful, one-year-old, blue Volkswagen convertible, which had just had a complete check-up. We got to the church on time but, as I was parking my car in the church parking lot, the clutch felt kind of funny. At least it had never acted that way before. I couldn't imagine starting on a seven-week honeymoon without having it checked. But it was Saturday! Could a Volkswagen mechanic be found? With these unsettling thoughts circulating in my mind, I entered the church, hardly able to concentrate on what was about to take place.

The wedding began on time but as Sue (who never looked lovelier) and I stood at the altar facing the priest, we noticed a look of annoyance on his face as he beckoned the altar boy to come to him. The boy hadn't brought the prayer book used in conducting weddings and the priest was unable to start the ceremonies without it. As the harried kid searched for the right book, a good deal of time was consumed. The delay gave the priest a good chance to do some ad-libbing and he did a most commendable job.

Finally, when the proper book was found, the ceremonies began. How beautiful they were! Sue and I were truly touched. I was particularly impressed with the organist, whose playing gave me goose bumps. Since the ceremonies included a nuptial mass, the wedding was longer than the average one, but the time seemed to fly.

At the wedding's conclusion, my new bride and I floated down the aisle, courtesy of cloud nine. My state of ecstasy was such that, as I was standing outside the church immediately following the wedding, I kissed the first person I saw, my wife's Uncle Mannie!

The reception was held at the home of Sue's parents. A good time was had by all, but I couldn't help wondering what that funny feel to the car's clutch was all about. My brother-in-law, Tom, wasn't able to locate a Volkswagen mechanic but he did find a repair shop where the clutch was checked. He returned with the happy news that the problem was minor and the car could be driven for many miles before repairs would become necessary.

The reception no sooner ended than fate ordained that this happiest day of our lives should include a comic touch. As I was driving back to my in-laws' house after a quick trip to the bus depot, my car suddenly started losing power. It would then regain power only to lose it again. I began wondering what kind of servicing the car had received at the repair shop. That morning it was the clutch, and now this! Had someone played the practical joke of all practical jokes and sabotaged my car on my wedding day?

Managing to get the car to within half a mile of my destination, it finally gave up the ghost. I pushed the car over to the curb, whipped out a cigarette, and smoked to beat the band as I hustled over to the nearest phone booth which was, of course, occupied. I pictured Sue wondering where in heaven's name I could be.

At long last, the phone was mine. Quickly I explained to my wife that our car, which had so recently been given a clean bill of health, appeared to be definitely ill, so much so that it wouldn't move. I asked her to get some help. In a flash I saw my wife's Uncle Chet in his pickup, heading my way. But he didn't notice me or the car and passed right by. I moaned! We should be headed for our honeymoon, I thought, and here I am playing games on South Main Street in Salinas!

There was no long wait for Chet to find me. In a jiffy he was back ... saying he'd been daydreaming. He attached a heavy rope to the car's front bumper and pulled me to my in-laws' house. While we all sat around the house wondering why the car wouldn't start, Chet, just for laughs, asked me if there was any gas in the car. Gas? Gas—that had to be it!

The early Volkswagens didn't have a gas gauge, so every 250 to 275 miles, you'd have to remember to gas up. In case you forgot, the car would start losing power for lack of gas and do a kind of bunny hop as mine had just done. This problem was easily remedied by switching to the auxiliary tank, which provided an additional gallon of gasoline. Several times I'd had to make use of this spare gallon. But being very distracted that day, I completely forgot about it when the car started bunny hopping.

I raced out to the car, switched to the auxiliary tank, pressed down on the gas pedal a few times and then turned the key. On a dime the car started! And to think of all the time I'd wasted stuck on South Main Street.

Loading the car didn't take long. We said our good-byes and began an eventful seven-week, 14,000-mile honeymoon across the United States and Canada, which included twenty-five states and seven Canadian provinces. From the outset we wondered how long it would be before the clutch started acting up seriously enough to require repair work. It wasn't long before this concern was almost forgotten as we came face-to-face with a much more serious problem.

Crossing the Tehachapi Mountains, just out of Bakersfield, California, in 100-degree–plus weather, I made the mistake of driving too fast in second gear. Between the intense heat and the steepness of the grade, the pressure on the engine was too much. Something had to give ... and it did! All of a sudden ... Pow! Ping! Pang! Ting! Tung! Tang! Our beautiful, blue convertible sounded like the percussion section of some far-out musical group gone berserk! I immediately pulled over to the side of the road. At the same moment, the horrible racket ended and the engine quit. Inexplicably, neither of us was overly concerned. Was this show of bravery attributable to stupidity, ignorance, or just plain love? Very calmly we got out of the car and surveyed the situation ... which didn't look very encouraging. Then, just because I could think of nothing else to do, I turned the key in the ignition and the little German car started just like that! It was the very last thing that we expected it to do ... really. Which goes to show that the luck of the Irish isn't restricted to them.

With no more than a five-minute delay, we were on our way again, wondering how the car would handle the rugged driving ahead of us. At times, it gave signs of having lost some of its zip, but it made it over the Tehachapis and into the Mojave Desert, where in one place we noticed a reading of 120 degrees.

As we were zooming along at seventy miles per hour as if nothing had happened, without the slightest warning the wild drummers came back for an encore. The scene was a repetition of the first one, except that neither Sue nor I bothered to get out of the car this time. And when some guys in a California Highway Department truck stopped to ask if we needed assistance, we politely turned down their offer. Ever since that day I've wondered many times how we were able to exhibit such confidence that we wouldn't be stuck out there in the desert. With the tremendous heat, the situation could have become dangerous if the car had decided not to start. As in the first case, though, within five minutes, the car started on the first try.

Our happiness and puzzlement can be readily imagined as we again whizzed along at seventy miles per hour. How could anything be seriously wrong with our car if it could run so smoothly? On the other hand, how could it be in sound condition if it had twice performed its drumming act and quit for five-minute rest periods? To our great relief, however, the drumming and quitting routines ceased.

The tiny, blue Volks fairly flew across Arizona and New Mexico, as pretty as you please, until we reached Tucumcari, New Mexico. At that point, whatever was supposed to eventually happen to the clutch happened. Shifting gears then had to be accomplished without benefit of the clutch ... which was most unhealthy for both our nerves and the car's gears.

The closest Volkswagen dealer was in Amarillo, Texas, a 112-mile trip. It was our great fortune that this road was flat, without any towns, stoplights, or even stop signs. While driving through Tucumcari, I shifted gears as little as possible. The grinding sounds were both awful and embarrassing. Once out of town, we went directly to the outskirts of Amarillo without ever having to change gears.

The next morning we had to drive to downtown Amarillo to get to the Volkswagen dealer. I used second gear all the way. The clutch was repaired quickly and at little expense. But, almost as an afterthought, the mechanic told us that further work was needed on our car. When he described the condition of the engine—one broken piston, two scoured cylinders, etc., etc., etc.—our shock was all too apparent. We now clearly understood why the car had sounded so terrible on the two occasions when it had broken down. I asked the man when the repairs could be made. He didn't get a chance to finish the word *tomorrow,* because it was drowned out by my pleas for mercy, which focused on the fact that this was our honeymoon.

I assured him that Amarillo was a gorgeous town but that we needed to get to New York. It must have been quite a performance because by five o'clock that afternoon, the work was completed and we were headed east, barely outracing a storm that gave Amarillo plenty of headaches. To this day, my wife and I have marveled at how that car of ours was able to drive like a dream all the way from the Mojave Desert of California to Amarillo, Texas, in spite of having the equivalent of a fractured skull!

With our car functioning properly, the rest of our honeymoon was serene. A great deal of time was spent in New York City visiting my relatives and friends and showing off my new bride. It was lots of fun for me to take Sue on a tour of New York's great sights, some of which I'd never seen myself!

We headed home via Canada, doing some camping along the way. By the time we reached the Canadian Rockies, we were so saturated with beautiful scenery it was difficult to appreciate the most spectacular scenery of the whole trip.

Within a few days, our lengthy journey came to an end as we arrived in Salinas, so glad to be home.

Chapter Six

It's Carrot, Not Car Rot

"Boys and girls, June is just around the corner. It'll be here before you know it." This being the first day of school, I'm sure that my optimism wasn't shared by the majority of my students. As usual I went over the class rules, making them as clear as possible, emphasizing the fact that I was saying what I meant, and meaning what I said.

Now, any teacher likes to be obeyed. Who wouldn't agree with that? But when a student is obedient to the point of ridding his stomach of its contents on the classroom floor rather than leaving his seat without the teacher's permission, it's time for a better explanation of the rules.

I'd been faced with this particular situation the previous year, after which I went through the process of explaining how this distressing experience need not happen again. Wishing to avoid a repeat performance during the current year, I made it abundantly clear to the class that if anyone needed to use the lavatory in an emergency, for the love of himself, the janitor, his classmates and me, he should leave his seat and the room on the double, without even thinking of asking for my permission. I stressed "without even thinking of asking for my permission," hoping to make the point perfectly clear.

My students apparently got the message. On those rare occasions when a student would suddenly make a mad dash for the lavatory, I'd sincerely hope that his arrival was well timed. Down through the years, on opening day I've always stated: "If you've got to go, just go, and don't even think of asking." Who knows how much embarrassment that simple statement has saved.

The staff preparation days held prior to the opening of school are usually busy-but-calm days. Often included in the doings is a breakfast or luncheon sponsored by the PTA or some other organization. There are staff meetings, at which time new members are introduced and school policies discussed. Much of the time, though, is spent checking out books and supplies and prettying up the classrooms for the children's arrival.

This particular year the staff preparation days were destined to be unforgettable. In fulfillment of the fondest wishes of the majority of the student body, one of the large buildings on campus caught fire and was slightly damaged, mostly by smoke and water. Although the fire caused extra work for the staff, the educational process wasn't hampered in the least. The classes scheduled to be conducted in the damaged building were held there just as planned, much to the disappointment of many students.

If I had to choose one year in which I showed the most growth in teaching techniques, it would have to be this, my second year at Freedom. How do you help a child improve his reading skills when he's in sixth grade and barely able to read from one of those *Dick and Jane* first grade readers? Do you ask him to read from a sixth grade reader, all the while reading for him each word he gets stuck on, which will probably be about ninety percent of the words? Or do you employ this same method using a first grade reader, in which case the reading will be much easier, with the child needing fewer words read for him? How about having him memorize each word in his reader, so that whenever he sees a word he has committed to memory, he'll be able to recognize it by its appearance and read it? Or would it be preferable to go the phonics route, teaching him to sound out words?

When I'd first tried my hand at remedial reading a few years before, the student I was attempting to help was a seventh grader reading at about the second grade level. I tried the "read for him each word he can't read" method, using both seventh and second grade readers. The results were dismal. He'd get stumped over and over again on the same words I'd read for him repeatedly. Whatever gains were made, if any, had to have been mostly by chance.

Despite the failure of this unimaginative, primitive, and unproductive approach to remedial reading, I persisted in using it whenever there was an unfortunate kid in dire need of help. The results were always seemingly negligible.

At the beginning of the year, it was decided by the four of us sixth grade teachers to divide our classes into four reading groups based on reading ability. The top group included some readers at the eighth grade level, while in the bottom group, most of the students were only able to read a second grade reader at best. Each of us selected a reading group. I chose the bottom one. It was the challenge I was looking for. Somehow I'd find a way to teach these poorest of readers to read much better.

My group had thirty students, which was far too many for a remedial reading class. Once I heard them read, I felt that a second grade reader wouldn't be too easy or too difficult for any of the kids. So each of these sixth graders started off the year with a second grade reader. For sure, there was nowhere else to go but up! Everyone got a turn at reading aloud each day. If a student was unable to read a word, I'd never read it for him. Instead, I would provide him with help in sounding it out—the phonics approach.

Let's go back over twenty years for an example. Margie is trying to read the following: Linda sees her dog down the street. Margie does fine until she comes to the word *street;* then she's stuck. What kind of help do I give her so that she's able to read the word on her own?

There are various approaches. Here are two. The first is to break down the word. I ask her if she sees any word or words in the word *street.* If she answers *tree,* then I ask her to add the *T* sound to the word *tree,* in which case Margie will most likely say, *treet.* All right, now I ask her to blend the *S* sound with *treet.* If done properly, she'll recognize the word as *street.*

But suppose she isn't capable of blending the *S* sound with *treet.* No big problem exists. Because she's gotten as far as *treet,* I ask Margie to read the sentence, and when she reaches the word she can't read, to just say *treet.* As the kid reads the sentence, Linda sees her dog down the *treet,* the chances are excellent that she'll recognize what the word should be, and say *street.*

Spending all this time with the word *street,* Margie shouldn't have much, if any, trouble reading the word the next time she runs across it. And think of how much the rest of the class has been learning while Margie and I have been playing around with sounds!

Travis is trying hard to read this sentence: The air is clean. He's really stumped because he can't read the words *air* or *clean.* Again I have a choice of ways to help without reading the words for him.

One method is to construct sentences using *air* and *clean* until the words are found which will enable Travis, through association, to solve his problem. Here are four examples of sentences I can use: You need air in the tire. The kite is way up in the air. My hands are dirty so I will clean them. Clean the mud off the boots.

Travis shouldn't have any trouble reading the two words now, not with these sentences, which are not only simple, but contain words the child will be inclined to associate with *air* and *clean*.

Another approach is through rhyming. I can make the word *air* easier by building other words from it. The words *fair, hair* and *pair* give Travis three chances to figure out how to read *air*. These words can be put into simple sentences, as in the previous method, if he can't read any of them. As long as Travis is able to read just one of those words, chances are he'll be able to read all of them and have little or no difficulty in reading *air* because eliminating the first letter of *fair, hair,* or *pair* will give him the word *air*.

The word *clean* is simplified by dropping the first letter so that you have *lean*. If Travis can't read the shorter word, I must then try words that rhyme with it such as *bean, Jean,* or *mean*. If that isn't effective, I'll again construct simple sentences out of the rhyming words, which should do the trick. Once Travis is able to read the word *lean,* adding the letter *C* to *lean* makes it easy for him to say *clean*.

There was one reading period that year during which I spent more than ten minutes helping Willie to read the word *carrot*. Wow! By the time he was able to read that word, I'd used up so much energy in guiding him along I was exhausted ... but thoroughly happy.

At the conclusion of this exercise in verbal calisthenics, the blackboard was chock-full of sentences and rhyming words, all aimed at helping Willie with the word *carrot*. I can still see the words *car, bar, far, jar, tar,* along with *dot, got, hot, jot, lot, not, pot, rot, tot,* written on the board. Also clearly pictured are sentences such as these three: Bunny eats a carrot. Willie went to the garden to get a carrot. A carrot is orange in color. Would you believe that the very next day, when I asked him to read the word on which we'd spent more than twenty percent of a reading period, he couldn't do it? But this time it only took me a minute to help him read the word.

After the class completed the second grade reader, the students had to be able to read the word list in the back of the book before being advanced to the third grade reader. This was the true test of how much their reading had improved because reading isolated words is more difficult than reading these same words when they're contained in a story, where other words and pictures can be helpful.

The same procedure was followed upon completion of the third grade reader. As the year progressed, it became less necessary to help kids read words, even though the reading matter became increasingly difficult. By the end of the year this remedial class was reading smoothly from a fourth grade reader, and I was tickled pink!

My regular class consisted of thirty-six children, which was the largest group I'd taught since my first year of teaching back in The Bronx. In that second year at Freedom School, I don't think it would have bothered me even if there had been fifty kids in my class. Oh, was I motivated! Those boys and girls simply *had* to learn, because I *had* to teach! Certainly, being happily married and expecting our first child in May contributed to my enthusiasm. And this enthusiasm must have been highly contagious because this class produced work of such rare quality that I began recording their class averages in spelling, social studies, and math. When they were consistently averaging over 90 percent in spelling, I asked them to do the "impossible," which involved achieving a class average of 100 percent in that subject!

Now, to ask all thirty-six children in a class to get 100 percent in a test of any kind might seem unrealistic, but they'd already come very close with 95 percent and 96 percent averages in spelling. So the big day came. The spelling test was made up of twenty-four words, as usual. As I read the words from the speller, it was easy to see the look of concentration on their faces as they carefully wrote each word. At the end of the test, I chose to correct the papers right then and there. While the tests were being corrected, the room was almost as silent as if it were empty, with the kids anticipating the results with bated breath. When I told them that there were two 92s and the rest of the papers were 100s, they were disappointed, but had the decency not to ask the names of the two students who missed getting 100 percent.

I heartily congratulated this great bunch of kids, assuring them that a 99 1/2 percent class average in spelling wasn't too shabby! Their reward for such a remarkable achievement, besides oodles of praise, was one hour of recess ... immediately!

The social studies class averages were great, too, usually in the upper 80s. But with so much subject matter to be covered and the wide range in IQs, trying for a 100 percent class average was never seriously considered.

Regarding math, there seemed to be an 80 percent math barrier. Each exam brought many 100s, 90s, and 80s, but also enough low grades to prevent the average from ever reaching 80 percent or better. I felt it was time for this barrier to be broken.

One day I decided to supermotivate. By this I mean *a la* Knute Rockne in the Notre Dame locker room at halftime, getting his players all fired up and asking them to "win one for the Gipper." With as much drama as my ham nature could produce, I told the kids that against them the 80 percent math barrier didn't stand a chance. At the same time it was made clear that just a few low grades such as 50 percent, 40 percent, or worse, could mean defeat. I finished my pep talk by letting them know that the reward for victory, aside from a sense of pride in accomplishment, was a huge amount of recess.

In preparation for the big test, I spent much time giving extra help to those who had already been receiving special attention. Following some final advice on the importance of checking their work and not rushing, I gave the test. It was made up of ten multiplication examples—375 x 45, 680 x 57—that sort of thing. Those kids worked ever so carefully ... and accurately. And success was theirs, just barely, with a class average of exactly 80 percent. My Rockne "go get 'em" speech had worked! For the rest of that year, class averages of 80 percent and over became common in math.

With all these exciting breakthroughs, teaching had become so thrilling that each afternoon, as soon as I got home from school, I'd give Sue a full run-down on the events of the day. Just as in the previous year, she'd been introduced to my class and had spent a day observing these "wonder kids" at work. On this occasion, though, since Sue was in a family way, she refrained from racing any of the kids, which would have been a bit much.

The purpose of introducing Sue to my students each year was simple. With the kids and I being such good friends, why not have them meet my best friend, the one they'd hear so much about during the year? In this way it would be easier for them to appreciate her. Also, when I babbled like a brook about Deborah, Buddy, Kathy, Pete, or Whoever, it would be meaningful to Sue. Still there were times when it was pretty tough for her to put faces and names together.

Speaking of Pete, a short time ago, while walking across South Main Street in Salinas, I just happened to glance at a young gentleman also making his way across that busy thoroughfare. Our eyes met and I said, "You've got to be Pete Ortega." Instantly he replied, "Mr. Sorgi." It had been sixteen or seventeen years since we'd seen each other. With lots of laughs, we reminisced about sixth grade. Pete mentioned how much he'd enjoyed school that year, which, of course, didn't make me feel overly rotten! When I told him I was in the process of writing a book on my teaching experiences, he asked me if he was going to be in it. I assured him that his name would find its way into my book.

Pete had some time to spare so, naturally, I hustled him over to the house to show Sue "what" I'd found! Unfortunately, she was out shopping. Like all good things, this wonderful little reunion ended too soon, for Pete had to get back to work.

When Sue got home I told her that I'd bumped into one Pete Ortega and the name meant something to her. If I had never bothered to introduce her to the kids down through the years I believe that Sue, the kids, and I would have missed out on many heartwarming experiences.

"What Happened to Lincoln's Body?" This was the title of a story featured in *Life* magazine, February 15, 1963. On the cover, just below the title, was a very faded photograph of a coffin-shaped box being handled by a group of men. Never before or since have I been more anxious to learn the answer to a question. Anything concerning our sixteenth president has always drawn my attention.

I wondered what could possibly have happened to Lincoln's body! Wasn't it placed in a coffin and interred in a huge tomb in Illinois? Upon reading this incredible story, I was amazed not only at its contents, but also by the fact that it hadn't become a well-known part of Lincoln's biography.

Constantly on the lookout for stories to share with my kids, I felt I'd really struck a bonanza with this one. The next day my class was told they were going to hear a story to beat all stories ... and that it was long and kind of spooky, to boot. The kids were joyous—no school work for a while, and, as if that weren't enough, they were going to have the opportunity of being delightfully frightened. Wow, what a tough combination to beat! Happiness was theirs.

So that the kids might better appreciate the story they were about to hear, I spent considerable time talking about slavery, the Civil War, Lincoln's family, the assassination plot, and finally, the shooting of Lincoln. At the children's request, the lights were now turned off, an important preliminary to hearing any scary story. And in a classroom not quite dark enough to suit them, this is what they heard.

In 1876, eleven years after Lincoln was buried at Oak Ridge Cemetery in Springfield, Illinois, thieves broke into the tomb of the Lincoln Monument and almost succeeded in stealing his body. But, by chance, the Secret Service had found out about the plot, followed the criminals to the cemetery and arrested them in the act of lifting the president's coffin out of the white marble sarcophagus in which it had been placed. They'd planned to insist on $200,000 for the return of Lincoln's body.

With this incident in mind, some of Lincoln's friends hid the coffin between the walls of the tomb, and for years visitors paid their respects to an empty sarcophagus. In 1900 it was decided that the original Lincoln Monument had to be demolished and rebuilt. While the monument was under reconstruction, the bodies of Lincoln, his wife, three sons and grandson were secretly buried nearby.

When the new monument was completed, the six bodies were removed from their temporary grave and deposited in the tomb. Lincoln's body was placed in the same sarcophagus from which the thieves had almost stolen it. As a security measure, the authorities ordered a burglar alarm to be installed between the tomb and the custodian's home a few hundred feet away.

Despite this new protective device, Lincoln's only surviving child, his eldest son, Robert, was dissatisfied, feeling that his father's body could still be stolen from its tomb. So he gave new directions, ordering the construction crew to first make a hole ten feet deep in the tile floor of the tomb. The coffin was then to be placed in a steel cage resting on twenty inches of concrete at the bottom of this hole. Finally, concrete would be poured on the coffin and cage, binding them together into a solid block of rock.

On Thursday, September 26, 1901, all was ready. Twenty people gathered at the monument. They were state officials and members of the Lincoln Guard of Honor, a local group of men. There were also two women present. It wasn't long until an argument began. Should the coffin be opened to make certain it was really Abraham Lincoln who was being buried? The coffin had last been opened in 1887. Because of constant rumors across the country that Lincoln was not in that coffin, most of those present thought it would be a good idea to open it. Those opposed to the idea stated that Robert Lincoln had made it plain that he didn't want the casket opened, and he was the only person who had the right to say yes or no.

At long last it was decided that the coffin should be opened. Two plumbers were summoned to chisel an oblong piece out of the top of the lead-lined coffin, just over Lincoln's head and shoulders. These same men had opened the casket in 1887.

Joseph Lindley, a member of the Lincoln Guard of Honor sent a message to his thirteen-year-old son, Fleetwood, to ride out to the tomb as quickly as possible. He wanted the boy to have an unforgettable experience.

As Fleetwood furiously pedaled the two miles from school, he wondered what could be important enough for him to be excused from class by his teacher. Arriving at the tomb, the answer was clear. He knew what he was going to see.

Suddenly all was still. The coffin was opened as the oblong section of green-colored lead was lifted from above Abraham Lincoln's head and chest. A pungent, frighteningly suffocating odor arose. All twenty-three persons were drawn closer to the casket. The dark brown face of Lincoln had a thick covering of white chalk that had been applied by an undertaker in Philadelphia in 1865 on the westward trip, after Lincoln's skin had mysteriously turned black. Lincoln's face, as a result, took on the appearance of powdered bronze. The features were definitely Lincoln's and his expression was one of sadness. The headrest was not in its proper place, so the neck was thrown back. But the chin whiskers were perfect. The black bow tie, the wart on his cheek, the coarse, black hair all were unmistakable. The eyebrows, though, had vanished. The suit was covered with tiny bits of yellow mold. In addition there were red spots that looked like bits of material, possibly from a small American flag that had rotted away. Over his hands were what remained of the French kid gloves the president had been buried in.

All agreed beyond a doubt, it was Abraham Lincoln. The cut out piece was resoldered and then Robert Lincoln's directions were carried out. The coffin was lowered into the cage and two tons of concrete poured down, rolling and lapping about the metal. President Lincoln is still there, ten feet beneath the floor, and since that day in 1901, millions of people have visited his tomb.

As for Fleetwood Lindley, the bicycle boy, he was seventy-five when he recounted the scene to a *Life* reporter while in a Springfield hospital awaiting a gallbladder operation. Yes, he'd never forgotten that day. The reporter interviewed Fleetwood Lindley just in time because three days later, on February 1, 1963, he died—the last of the twenty-three who could say, "I saw him."

Since practice makes perfect and most California kids have twelve months in which to play baseball, it's not surprising that good baseball players and California are synonymous. At Freedom School, baseball received a boost in the form of all-star games. Fifth grade teacher, Owen Hand, originated the idea by offering to pit his stellar performers against mine. Upon carefully weighing the pros and cons of such a confrontation for precisely one second, I agreed wholeheartedly.

Once a week the big game took place. Owen and I would take turns pitching for both teams. Just because my kids were sixth graders didn't guarantee victory over Owen's younger guys. The games were mostly close but the sixth grade team did have an edge in the number of games won.

The one annoying thing about these games was the way in which some of the students, to get a better view of the action, would stand very close to the third base line. This practice could be dangerous to life and limb. Third base is called "the hot corner" for good reason. Many line drives whistled down the line, barely missing kids who weren't paying close enough attention to the game. Time after time students were told to move back. This they did. But unconsciously they'd work their way back to the line.

Finally it happened. One of the boys got nailed, but good, right on the jaw with a solid line drive ... which extracted one of his teeth just as pretty as you please! Luckily, the balls we used were not as hard as regular baseballs, otherwise he might have had real problems.

On the subject of baseball-related injuries: they were common enough to make me paranoid about safety. Some kids would throw the bat wildly in the direction of the catcher after hitting the ball and heading toward first base. This action sometimes necessitated a trip to the nurse's office for the poor catcher.

One morning just before classes began, I saw a distracted kid get clobbered in the arm as he walked into a swinging bat. No sooner did the little guy start howling than he was joined by a boy who got hit on the right side of his head by a ball, thrown at very close range ... which has got to be one of the less desirable methods of acquiring a headache! To this day, I never swing a bat unless I look behind me first just to make sure nobody has decided to materialize there.

In April, Sue and I moved into our first home, which, due to its shape and color, vaguely resembled navy barracks. It was in excellent condition and furnished but in desperate need of an exterior color change and some interior redecorating. Situated on a huge lot with a countrified atmosphere with a peek at Monterey Bay, this diamond in the rough became ours for what today would be merely a downpayment: $13,250.

By the time we finished jazzing up the place, it no longer looked plain, especially when topped off with an elegant, beveled-glass lantern over the front door. I always insisted that this light fixture increased the house's value by at least a thousand dollars. Now our home took on a colonial appearance, which was the general idea.

Our older daughter, Anne Elizabeth, made her debut on May 11th, rather interesting when you consider that Sue's birthday and mine fall on May 9th and May 12th, respectively. That year, May 12th was also Mother's Day. So between all sorts of greeting cards, presents, and cigars, it was indeed a costly week ... and has been ever since!

When I got to school on Monday morning, the kids were very happy to hear that I'd become a proud papa. The first thing they did was write messages of congratulations on the blackboard. Then came many questions concerning the new baby and Sue. It was anything but your average school day. In the few weeks of school that remained, there were many, much-appreciated gifts for Anne Elizabeth.

Earlier in the year I'd gone to San Francisco and collected about fifty gorgeous posters, mostly from airline and national tourist offices—all free. My classroom never looked so good! Because a picture is worth a thousand words, there was a pretty good social studies course to be had merely by looking at the posters on the walls.

Before my class left for summer vacation, I did a little gift giving myself. Each student received a poster from this large, colorful collection. Just prior to dismissal, the kids agreed unanimously that June had, indeed, arrived quickly!

Chapter Seven

Whistlin' Dixie

Mr. Sorgi,

There are two things I'm opposed to concerning my children's education: *waste* and *boredom!* From what I hear from my contemporaries, you are a fine educator and eminently qualified to provide Scott with the type of teaching he is entitled to. Both Mrs. Taylor and I are very strict disciplinarians. I offer you the privilege of dealing with my son in *any* way you deem fit to keep him in line. I appreciate the problems you have in dealing with a roomful of small incendiaries. So much for the preamble!

Last evening Scott showed me a list of twenty words that he was assigned to copy thirty-five times each. I took that list, Mr. Sorgi, and using all the devious methods I could muster up, had Scott spell them for me. He spelled every one correctly and without hesitation. Against his wishes I told him to forget the *lines*. He still insisted on doing them. I admire his respect for you.

I do not admire the assignment. I received my doctorate of lines at E.A. Hall and graduated

97

magna cum laude. They didn't kill me physically but the *waste* and *boredom* was slow in healing. Please, if Scott misbehaves (and he's an *odds-on* favorite) and it is your judgment to punish him with lines—*do it,* but *not with words he knows.* Challenge him, too. Why not have him copy the Bill of Rights, the various sections of our Constitution, the Magna Carta, the Gettysburg Address?

May I hear from you?

Regards,
Ted T. Taylor

If there were a Nobel Prize for notes sent to teachers, this masterpiece of diplomacy would surely be an odds-on favorite to win! My initial reaction, however, was lacking in enthusiasm. I wasn't overly fond of being hit, first thing, by the words *waste* and *boredom*—words that I found hurtful. But after rereading the note, it was obvious that Ted Taylor not only had a legitimate gripe that must be coped with, but was also gifted with a gentle, persuasive touch. And when I met Ted, it was plain to see that the note was indelibly stamped with his attractive personality.

I received this note a few weeks after the opening of the new Freedom School, which had been built a very short distance from the old one. While it was under construction, I'd heard many comments about its progressive design, yet had never bothered to find out exactly where the school was being built. When I first saw it, I wasn't too wild about its ultramodern appearance, as exemplified by the roof, which strongly resembled an open accordion. But on seeing just a few of the conveniences that the new school offered, I decided I could live with this roof—a roof so strange that, in all probability, every bird with an eye for beauty would studiously avoid landing on. As a nature lover, all I'd have to do would be to make a concerted effort to convince myself that the accordion-like roof was, in reality, a rugged mountain range. And if, by chance, my imagination wasn't up to performing such mental gymnastics, I could simply ignore this architectural blemish.

I was continually searching for challenges, but my search ended almost before it began. For among my thirty-two sixth graders were two nonreaders who could barely read a word. It was clear that they would require much more help than could be given to them during regular class time. So for many an after-school session, these two intelligent kids, who for some reason hadn't learned to read, spent time with me, gradually acquiring this most necessary skill. By June they were reading at the third grade level and feeling a lot better about themselves.

One of the meanings of the verb *to enrich* is to supply with anything, such as knowledge, in abundance. As I came to the conclusion that kids are capable of learning much more than is generally expected of them, I proceeded to offer my class the opportunity to become whiz kids ... genuine walking encyclopedias. And they accepted my offer with much gusto.

In addition to their regular subjects, I planned to provide them with a study of the presidency, plus the geography of the United States. Even the world champion bookworm couldn't deny that this would be an abundant supply of knowledge for any sixth grade class.

For just a moment or two, then, let's go back a couple of decades and listen in on a typical question-and-answer period to see what this enrichment program produced. Following each question, just imagine seeing most hands raised and hearing me being "Mr. Sorgiized" continually as the children compete with one another to answer the questions.

"Who was the first president to die in office and for how long was he president? ... Ken."

"William Henry Harrison ... one month."

"Terrific, Ken! Okay, who was the heaviest president and how much did he weigh? As a matter of fact, this man was so large that a special bathtub had to be installed for him in the White House. ... Duane."

"William Howard Taft and he weighed over 300 pounds."

"You're great, Duane! What president had a bullet near his heart that couldn't be removed? I'd also like to know how the bullet got there. I hope no wise guy tells me it arrived at the spot via a gun! ... Nancy."

"Andrew Jackson. He was shot in a duel."

"Fantastic, Nancy! Next question. Who was the first president to live in the White House? ... Toni."

"That's easy. John Adams."

"Oooo, how marvey, Toni! A minute ago I asked you superkids for the name of the largest president. Now can any cool cat tell me who the smallest president was? He was just a little, itsy-bitsy guy. ... Carol."

"James Madison."

"Hey, Carol, you're getting to be so smart you might just as well take over and do the teaching. All right, here's a good one. What president sent the 'Great White Fleet' around the world to show off American naval power? ... Rhoda."

"Theodore Roosevelt."

"Rhoda, you're beautiful! Okay, now for just a few questions on the fifty states. Question number one. ... What's the name of the highest mountain in the United States? ... Scott."

"Mr. Sorgi, that's so easy. ... Mount McKinley."

"Neato, Scott! Is there a miniature genius who can tell me where the Keys are located? And I don't mean my car keys, either. ...Larry."

"The Keys are in Florida."

"You're right, as usual, Larry! I'd now like to know in which state the Mississippi River has its source. ... Debbie."

"It's in Minnesota."

"Jazzy, Debbie! Here's a question that might stump a lot of you. In which state is the geographical center of the United States located? ... Jimmy."

"In Kansas."

"Wow, Jimmy, that's nothing short of superb! And now to conclude this quiz. What city is famous for the manufacture of musical instruments? ... Verna."

"Elkhart."

"Ah, that's music to my ears, Verna! Well, the recess bell is going to ring in about a minute, so let's get ready to go out. You know, class, I'm so impressed with your responses this afternoon that I feel you've earned an extra fifteen minutes of recess."

Praise—who can ever get too much of that wonderful stuff? I've always lavished it on my students as if there might not be a tomorrow! There are many reasons for which a child can be praised and they needn't have anything to do with schoolwork. For example, Judy comes to school with a new jacket. How easy it would be to make her day with a remark such as: Hey, Judy, I love that jazzy jacket. It makes you look absolutely gorgeous!

One of my favorite compliments goes like this: Mike, I'm totally wild about that shirt you're wearing. May I have it? I'll give you my shirt and throw in the tie for good measure. How does that deal grab you, pal?

Then there's praising a child just because he exists: Pat, you're a terrific guy. You can't imagine how happy I am to have you in my class!

Along the same line, it would be a cinch to boost Kathy's ego by saying, Kathy, if you become any prettier, you're going to take off and fly around like an angel!

Finally there are those children who are in desperate need of praise. As I put my arm around a friendless or homely student and tell her she's a marvey girl and a very important member of our class, her self-image is on its way to a change for the better. Inviting a problem kid for a game of catch and complimenting him on whatever ability he shows will surely be a step in establishing rapport.

All of this praise conveys love, and love goes a long way toward creating a happy classroom environment. According to research it even helps raise children's IQs.

Life could be described as a procession of days blending into one another. How comparatively few of them stand out in one's memory. For example, it would be impossible for me to remember what I did on even one of the many February 7ths or April 22nds I've lived through.

On the other hand, some days were destined to be permanently etched on the memories of all those old enough to remember. For those a little over fifty, the events of December 7, 1941, "a date which will live in infamy," cannot be forgotten. Ask persons over thirty about November 22, 1963, and chances are they'll be able to tell you precisely where they were and what they were doing when they heard the shocking news: "President Kennedy has been shot in Dallas!"

Beginning in 1835 when Richard Lawrence failed in an attempt to assassinate Andrew Jackson, a number of presidents (and even a former president and president-elect) have been attacked by various brands of fanatics. In Jackson's case, two guns misfired at very close range, and "Old Hickory," as our seventh president was called, actually helped chase his assailant, threatening to annihilate him with his cane. Lawrence was caught, and spent the remainder of his life in an insane asylum.

Between 1865 and 1901, three presidents were gunned down. Sixteen years after Lincoln's murder, James Garfield was shot in the back at a Washington railroad depot by a man who'd been forever pestering him for a job. Garfield lived for a couple of months, while medical men tried in vain to remove the bullet from his body.

Only twenty years were to pass before another president was felled by an assassin's bullet. While shaking hands with visitors at the Pan-American Exposition in Buffalo, New York, William McKinley was fired at, point-blank, by an anarchist who held a gun concealed behind a handkerchief. McKinley died several days later.

And now, more than sixty-two years later, the fourth American president had just died violently. That cloudy Friday was the start of a dismally long weekend which, from beginning to end, seemed unreal—more so because it even included a killing seen live on television by millions of people.

I can still see myself starting to write the first example in a math test on the board. That's as far as I got. Suddenly the intercom came on, and over the radio my class and I heard the stunning news that President Kennedy had been shot.

Well, that took care of the test and also what remained of the morning. My class just sat—as still and wordless as statues—as I paced the floor. Reports came streaming in over the radio, but naturally, what was uppermost in our minds was whether the president was going to survive. We didn't have to wait long for the answer. Shortly before lunch we heard that John Fitzgerald Kennedy was dead.

Not much was said by either the kids or me. What could we say, all of us being in such a state of shock? We noticed some students passing our room crying and very shook-up. They ended up in the nurse's office trying to get hold of themselves.

The superintendent and the principal were fearful of this condition spreading. That's all the nurse would have needed—forty or fifty hysterical kids in her office! But some-how, we all got through the day.

After lunch, I spent the afternoon reading my class some of Edward Rowe Snow's fantastic sea stories, a good way, I felt, to divert their attention from the horror story they'd heard that morning.

The following Tuesday (Monday having been declared a national day of mourning), the kids and I decided to write letters of sympathy to Jacqueline Kennedy and also to the late president's parents, Joseph and Rose Kennedy. The sentiments expressed by the class were simple ... and priceless. How I wish I had kept copies of those letters! One in particular stands out in my memory. It was written by Kenny, using the best adjective he could come up with to describe his feelings on hearing the dreadful news. The word he chose was *stoned,* but to the best of my knowledge it didn't have any connection with drugs back in those more innocent days.

In class, I'd occasionally use the word *stoned* to describe a state of utter shock, rendering one immobile ... like a stone statue. I might say: When I saw the car pass me at well over 100 miles per hour, I was stoned. Well, Ken did his very best to express his feelings, and he believed that the word *stoned* described them perfectly. So he wrote something like this:

> Dear Mrs. Kennedy,
> I was sorry to hear what happened to your hus-band. When I heard the news I was stoned!
> Sincerely,
> Kenny

Jacqueline Kennedy replied to our letters with a note of appreciation addressed to the class and me. From Palm Beach, Florida, the Joseph Kennedys sent thank-you notes to each of us.

I've just finished a phone conversation with one of the all-star members of that class of twenty-odd years ago, Duane Loftin, a super guy. I asked Duane what was the first thing that came to his mind when he thought of sixth grade. His answer was instantaneous: the Kennedy assassination. Not far behind, but in great contrast to that awful day in November, 1963, was a hilarious episode that would be apt to stick in the mind of any student. It also occurred on a Friday ... and unexpectedly, too.

I'd given a math test and was hoping for good results ... like a class average in the 80s. One of my students (I'll call him Champy) informed me that he'd gotten 100 percent on the test. Now, because his chances of getting an A or even a B were slim, my reply was: "Champy, if you got 100, I'll stand on my head and whistle 'Dixie.' Of course, I'll also be deliriously happy." He then, with supreme confidence, let it be known that I'd better be prepared to do my stunt. I wondered how Champy could have possibly managed to get 100 percent in math, his weakness. How in blazes I'd ever perform my outlandish act didn't seem to concern me in the least. What excited me was the possibility of this struggling math student, who'd only dreamed of getting 100 percent, actually seeing his dream become a reality.

As I corrected his paper, I held my breath. My eyes raced back and forth between the answer sheet and his paper. All ten examples were correct! Fantastic! Terrific! Beautiful! Champy had scored 100 percent! He looked so happy, with an I-told-you-so expression all over his radiant face. My joy, of course, was also great, although I couldn't help wondering how the promised stunt could be pulled off successfully ... or even unsuccessfully, for that matter. Yet it was payoff time. The class was simply dying to watch me fulfill my end of the deal, without delay. Oh, they were excited! (I would have been infinitely more excited had my sixth grade teacher, a nun, been obliged to stand on her head and whistle anything!)

There was one rather important obstacle to my carrying out this circus act: I was incapable of standing on my head. Not at all surprisingly, the entire class was ready to render whatever aid might be needed. Quicker than a wink, I found myself upside down, the top of my head pressed lightly on the floor, my legs held straight up in the air by a multitude of overly enthusiastic kids. Try as I might, though, I couldn't whistle "Dixie" ... or anything else! All I could do was laugh, as whatever change was in my pockets cascaded to the floor.

Eventually my numerous helpers gently lowered me to the floor, in undamaged condition. What a fun experience it was for all of us, especially because it had been so spontaneous.

Which reminds me—What's spontaneous and can result in much "unfun"? How about spontaneous combustion? Every school has fire drills, but who ever expects them to be anything other than just that—drills? So when I stepped out of my classroom one morning and noticed smoke seeping out of the janitor's locked storeroom, my first thought was, Hey, I've discovered one of the rarest of phenomena. Next I recall thinking, How could anything have the gall to catch fire in a school, with all these kids around?

Telling my class to cool it, I rushed to the office and started to inform the district superintendent about the smoke. By the time I'd said *smo*— Noel Hubber was hot-footin' it (pun intended) to the storeroom with me in hot pursuit (pun also intended). If that fire had hoped to spread, it picked the dumbest of places to start: right next to a fire extinguisher. Noel no sooner saw the smoke than he became a most talented fire fighter, kicking in the glass to reach the extinguisher, unlocking the storeroom door, and spraying an oily mop which had been smoldering, ready to ignite. That took care of the fire danger.

In the meantime, the fire buzzer had gone off and hundreds of kids had been led briskly to the playground. The most dangerous part of this harmless incident, however, was the superintendent kicking in the little glass door to get the extinguisher. It could have been one of those look-Ma-no-foot deals. But he managed to limit the damage to a scuffed-up shoe.

The kindergarten teacher, Lucille Nielsen, thought I deserved some recognition for my role in preventing a "holocaust," so she presented me with a little, red, plastic fire hat ... just like those worn by her tiny kindergartners. Needless to say, I was considered hot stuff wearing it!

Children like gory stories and the history of Latin America glows red with incredible tales of bloodshed. The Aztecs of Mexico certainly produced an advanced civilization. Their chief city, Tenochtitlan, was a miracle of engineering that left the Spaniards awestruck. Yet, when it came to barbarism, these same Indians refined it to the point that it became, if you will, a "fine art."

Each year as many as 50,000 human beings, mostly war captives, were sacrificed. One very common sacrificial ritual was carried out in this manner: Atop a stone block, the victim was placed on his back in a spread-eagle position, with each of his limbs firmly grasped by a priest. A fifth priest held his head while another, the executioner, used an obsidian or flint knife to cut open the captive's chest. At this point his heart was torn out, held up toward the sun and then placed in a stone or wooden container. What a bloody mess it must have been!

But, oh, how the kids relished hearing this macabre and most unusual story. When, in this "Year of the New Freedom School," I retold the story for the umpteenth time, it proved to be more than one of the girls could take. Noticing some rapid movements in various directions toward the back of the room, I asked a simple question: "What happened?" The answer was equally simple, as a voice piped up, "She puked!" The poor kid got sick so suddenly she didn't even have a chance to make a mad dash for the rest room.

While on the subject of barbarism, here's another gruesome tale that was to become a favorite in future years. This story shows the Indian to be even more imaginative than in the previous heartbreaking account (pun intended).

The Spaniards had a perpetual case of gold fever. They were absolutely wild about gold and could never seem to get enough of it, tormenting the poor Indians mercilessly in their continuous quest for more and more of the precious yellow stuff. So what did a group of South American Indians do to a lone, captured Spaniard to "help" him satisfy his unquenchable thirst for gold? They most obligingly poured a "healthy" amount of it in molten form down the unlucky guy's throat!

Space limitation, an aversion to cruelty, and sympathy for my stomach do not permit me to go into the gory details of any of the tortures inflicted on the Indians by their numerous conquerors. Suffice it to say, in all fairness, no race has ever cornered the market on cruelty!

"Hey, Mr. Sorgi, did you hear the news? You won a contest! You're going on a trip to Japan, or somewhere around there!" Contest? Japan? What was Wade telling me, anyway? I couldn't remember entering any contest.

During the brief time required for that story to be straightened out, it was thrilling to hope that by some unprecedented stroke of luck, I was really going to Japan as the winner of a mysterious contest. But the truth of the matter was that I'd been nominated as one of many candidates in a "favorite teacher" contest. As far as winning anything, time would tell ... like about seven weeks.

The *San Jose Mercury-News* was sponsoring the contest. Close to 300 teachers had been selected. More than 200 of the nominees were from San Jose area schools. The remainder, like me, taught in schools averaging approximately fifty miles from San Jose, although two candidates had been chosen from as far away as Duluth, Minnesota, and Spokane, Washington. I never did find out, for certain, how a teacher was nominated. No matter. It was an honor and the prizes were enticing. First prize was a seven-week cruise to the Orient for two, plus a thousand dollars. The runner-up would win a jet trip to Britain for two, plus three hundred dollars. Not too shabby in the least!

The *Mercury-News* devoted a full page each day to advertising its contest. Among the items included in the ad were a complete list of the candidates and an official ballot. There was no limit to the number of times a person could vote, just as long as the official ballot was used. And, of course, each ballot was worth the price of one copy of the *Mercury-News*. A fair number of people in the Freedom-Watsonville area subscribed to this newspaper. But being realistic, I found it tough to imagine any teacher outside the San Jose area coming out on top. Yet, because the newspaper kept strictly mum on the results of the balloting, there was hope of victory ... and a dream of a trip for Sue and me.

My class worked hard to get votes. The kids collected ballots anywhere they could. As the weeks passed, I imagine that many a subscriber anxiously awaited the end of this newspaper game. One family managed, regularly, to accumulate a whole mess of newspapers, spending Sunday afternoons cutting out the ballots, which were filled in the next day by my class in an assembly-line manner.

In a show of remarkable fervor, Ken Mangan even decorated his lawn with a forest of signs pleading for all who might see his stirring display to "Vote for Mr. Sorgi." By the time the contest concluded on May 29th, my students had brought in upwards of five thousand ballots ... which was truly a colossal job!

However, on June 7th, when the winners were announced, those five thousand votes fell far short of sending me anywhere. As expected, both winners were from the San Jose area and had amassed many thousands of votes. I haven't the slightest doubt that their victories were well deserved.

What a marvey way to begin a summer vacation! I did go fishing in Idaho that summer.

Upper left: I finally took the plunge...figuratively...and learned to fly. Mom, my niece Margaret, and me.

Upper right: "Here are some pine cones...just for you, Mr. Sorgi." One half of my students at Lyman Springs School.

Lower left: Fishin' for compliments at recess, Lyman Springs School.

Lower right: With our car functioning properly, the rest of our honeymoon was serene.

Top: Freedom School, circa 1961. The building to the left of the cars contained the main teachers' lounge, where, periodically, soap operas were produced. Above: The new Freedom School, with its accordion-like roof. Lower left: The author standing in front of Adobe I. Lower right: Adobe II (actually, another almost identical adobe built several years later by my fourth grade in King City, California).

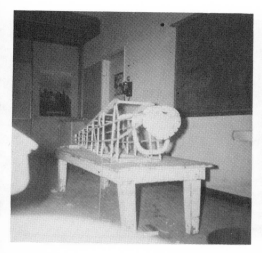 

Upper left: I chose to introduce my class to the art of balsa model airplane building.

Upper right: There wasn't even one outlandish bulge to be seen anywhere on the airplane. Part of my sixth grade class in the background.

Lower left: It came to roost in the cafeteria, rather elegantly perched upon several strands of heavy wire.

Lower right: In place of medals, each winner received a balsa model airplane which I'd built.

Above: At the completion of each Kingsley Frost "Carpentry Concerto" there'd be a sleek, thirty-five-foot fishing boat ready to be launched. Below: My sixth grade class and me on my last day at Yarmouth South Centennial School, June 20, 1969.

Chapter Eight

My Acapulco Dive

"Mr. Sorgi, after you fell, your face was as red as a beet and you looked so embarrassed!" During all my years of attending school I can't recall even one case of a teacher defying the law of gravity and losing so decisively as to end up sprawled on the floor like a rag doll. The dramatic flop I'd taken left my students stunned ... gazing at the scene in disbelief.

This unexpected plunge need not have occurred. It was brought about by my constant desire to provide descriptions more vivid than mere words could give. (How many times had I reenacted the role of John Wilkes Booth in the shooting of Abraham Lincoln—sound effects and all!)

In Acapulco, on Mexico's Pacific coast, there are some extremely rugged, rocky cliffs. From one of these cliffs, celebrated high divers leap into the sea 137 feet below. It is one of the most breathtaking of feats. Upon seeing this spectacular performance in a film, I could barely wait to tell my class about it. As I started describing this daring dive, with my feet planted firmly on the classroom floor, I sensed that a more descriptive setting was called for.

Just a few feet to my right was a classroom table whose legs were located toward its center rather than at the corners—not too safe a table to stand on, as I was about

111

to discover. The table was covered with a display of newly acquired science books, which deterred me not in the least. Enthusiastically stepping onto the edge of this table, I made like one preparing to go off a high diving board. Standing there describing in minute detail what I'd seen in the film, I suddenly found everything going every which way—a kind of localized earthquake! The table had unexpectedly tipped over, causing me to slide off inelegantly and land with my rear end on the floor and my legs up in the air! Carried along with me was an avalanche of books, which were scattered all over the place. Wow, what a scene! There I was on the floor with a classful of dumbfounded kids staring at me, all wondering what came next.

If I could have vanished instantly into thin air, that is exactly what would have come next. Not having this option, I got up hurriedly, gathered the books together and deposited them on that rotten table, resuming class as if—ha, ha, ho, hee—nothing had happened. But indeed, something had happened ... something enormously funny and immensely laughable! From a serious mood, the tone changed abruptly to one of great merriment as I started poking fun at my botched up demonstration. We all laughed to the point of exhaustion.

I wonder how many times the "Acapulco Dive" has been gleefully told and retold over the years by me and the students witnessing it? Also, being that stories lend themselves to much embroidery with the passage of time, it would be fascinating to hear various versions of this comical occurrence.

Within the first few weeks of the "Year of the Acapulco Dive," my enrollment had mushroomed to forty-one children. The classrooms at Freedom School certainly were not meant to hold such an awesome number of students. This fact was so plain to see that very soon six kids were transferred to one of the other schools in the district. Of the thirty-five who remained, there were more girls than boys, for a change.

Among the nineteen girls in that class was one who would prove to be a scholastic wonder. Out of approximately 125 tests given that year, only twice did Paula score less than 100 percent ... and it took until April for this to happen. The grades 94 and 90 looked out of place over Paula Kennedy's name. To date, no student I've taught has equaled her brilliant record of achievement. All right, Paula, wherever you are!

Remember Jack Armstrong, "The All-American Boy"? Well, Freedom School, Room 11, had its own version of that well-known young hero of yesteryear in the person of Wayne Parker. Let me tell you, this guy was the quintessence of masculinity, an eleven-year-old composite of Superman, John Wayne, and Daniel Boone. He possessed physical strength disproportionate to his years and he used it, fortunately, in a constructive manner. Just having Wayne around was a joy, for his helpfulness and courtesy knew no bounds.

When it came to fishing, hunting, camping, animal life, ranching—anything having to do with the great outdoors— his knowledge was phenomenal. Anytime we had a class discussion on a topic such as wildlife, it might have been to everyone's advantage for me to simply let Wayne take over the show.

One day while my superkid was attending instrumental music class, we were discussing weapons used in the Revolutionary War. I asked the class if anyone knew what grapeshot was. Nobody had even the slightest idea. As far as the kids were concerned, grapeshot could just as well have been grapes shot out of a gun in a moment of sheer desperation.

Preparing to give my class the answer, I noticed Wayne heading back to the classroom. Now I knew it wouldn't be necessary for me to provide the answer. Very quickly I told the kids that Wayne was coming and that, as he entered the room, I'd ask the question again. We all smiled and agreed that our expert would instantly and enthusiastically volunteer to supply us with an answer, which almost *had* to be correct.

The door was no sooner open than I "innocently" popped the question: "Does anyone know what grapeshot is?" Wayne stopped dead in his tracks and started waving a hand frantically ... sending the class and me into paroxysms of laughter and leaving him thoroughly puzzled! When I explained the reason for our wild outburst, Wayne, looking quite flattered, let it be known that grapeshot was grape-sized cannon shot used in the olden days.

To elaborate on his helpfulness and courtesy: Wayne was so helpful that he eventually conducted my physical education class in calisthenics at the end of each day, as I sat proudly watching his skillful demonstration. Wayne impressed people so much with his gentlemanly behavior that, during a visit to a bookshop with a few of his classmates while on a field trip, the proprietor presented him with a complimentary book as a token of appreciation for his outstanding courtesy. Wherever you happen to be, superguy, hip, hip hooray for Wayne Parker!

On first becoming acquainted with Dave Iermini, I had the feeling that within the decade spanned by his life, he'd already amassed enough knowledge to stand him in good stead for the rest of his days and then some. His mind was a finely tuned instrument of learning. Make no mistake about it, David's attitude seemed to be: you must teach, for I must learn. That suited me fine since, conversely, my feeling was: you must learn, for I must teach. If ever there were a meeting of minds in a teacher-student relationship, this was it.

As a bonus, Dave, like me, was an aficionado of baseball, an enthusiast with a vast storehouse of information on not only the current crop of ballplayers, but also on such stars as Babe Ruth, Ty Cobb, Walter Johnson, Tris Speaker, and a host of other immortals who made baseball history long before he was born.

One Sunday, David and his family treated me to a Giants–Houston doubleheader at San Francisco's Candlestick Park. What I remember most about that day was the sight of Masanori Murakami, the great pitcher from Japan, hurling for the Giants. Murakami sure had style! But unhappily for San Francisco, and joyfully for the rest of the National League, he returned to Japan after a short stay with the Giants.

Of all my memories of David Iermini, the one that I recall most fondly was his cute custom of notifying me by telephone—long distance, yet—of any television program he'd happen to be watching which he felt I'd enjoy. There always appeared to be a note of urgency in these phone calls. You'd have thought that dire consequences would have resulted from missing even one minute of the program. The conversations were brief, contained no small talk, and were limited to the bare essentials:

Me: "Hello."

David: "Mr. Sorgi, if you're not watching Channel 9, get it right away!"

Me: "What's on, Dave?"

David: "Get Channel 9 right away—terrific program. Bye."

Me: "Okay. Thanks. See ya."

It was as simple as that. Whenever this kid said that a program was terrific, you could be positive that it was. Sue and I still talk about a David-recommended production called "The Bold Ones," which featured a series of incredible acts of daring. In one of these acts, three skydivers go up in a light plane and prepare to do their act, which anyone but an angel would consider supergutsy, if not downright insane. For one of the three skydivers is parachuteless! That's correct ... *sans* parachute! And in this absurd condition he intends to hurl himself out of the plane and into a very wild, blue yonder!

He'll be preceded in this first-of-its-kind performance by his two cohorts. They will, through skillful maneuvering of their chutes, bring themselves, hopefully, into position to catch the guy ... who'll be plummeting, rocklike, toward the earth.

At a given signal, out jump the two skydivers wearing chutes, performing a sort of aerial ballet while trying to position themselves to catch their buddy. He then leaps out of the plane, plunging earthward, apparently headed for destruction. But miraculously, the timing is perfect and the three men meet in midair, descending gently to the good earth. What a sensational performance!

I saw David not very long ago in Santa Cruz where he was employed. We talked over old times and he gladly provided me with his impression of the Acapulco Dive. All I can say is, Dave, you're still beautiful. Thanks for the cherished memories.

On October 15, 1964, the New York Yankees lost the World Series to the St. Louis Cardinals, signaling the end of a dynasty which had lasted for more than forty years. On the following day, ten hours after the occurrence of this "world-shaking calamity," our younger daughter, Veronica Marie, hit the planet with the usual screaming and hollering that appears to be so much a part of this sort of thing.

When we took Ronnie home, her seventeen-month-old sister, Annie, had a look of joyful curiosity which seemed to say: Could this be a special kind of doll for me to play with ... one that keeps moving and making funny noises? How neat!

Maybe part of that look was due to the bizarre fashion in which my Aunt Mary had diapered her earlier in the day. By the time she was through attaching the diaper to Annie, the thing looked like a pair of loose trousers, utterly failing to serve the purpose for which it was intended. The resultant mess was quite "interesting."

I don't know what handing out cigars has to do with celebrating a baby's birth. Why not distribute avocados, pistachio nuts, or even cloves of garlic ... perish the thought! Anyway, I felt this custom should be observed.

After I announced to my students that over the weekend the Sorgi family had increased by one, each kid was given a big, fat cigar ... made of bubble gum. Now, as far as my class was concerned, Veronica's birth had become an occasion to remember.

It's always been fun telling students about my boyhood in the north Bronx. Those days were comparatively trouble-free and tame, although certain stories I related must have left them wondering just how far east the Wild West had extended! Case in point: "The Clorox Incident"—a dramatic and rather messy episode that was so unnecessary. As in many instances of bedlam and mayhem, it was a case of gradually rising tempers and then ... *poof* ... a whole series of things happening in a flash.

The main character in The Clorox Incident—a tall, friendly, easygoing guy whom I'll refer to as Tiny—was known as a gifted athlete. He was endowed with many skills, the most noticeable of which was the ability to throw a baseball with such force as to cause the catcher's hand to feel as if it had been struck by a cannonball. The trouble was that whenever the lean fireballer released one of his rocketlike pitches, there was serious doubt as to its ultimate destination. He'd played minor league ball and, with better control, might have made it to the big leagues, and possibly even stardom. (Remember what learning control did for Sandy Koufax?)

Well, it was about seven o'clock on a peaceful summer evening. A couple of my buddies and I were standing on the corner watching Tiny pitch to some hardy, brave soul across the street in a grassy area enclosed by a steel mesh fence. Another one of Tiny's friends, whom I'll call Buster, was viewing the pitching demonstration and apparently making remarks that Tiny wasn't too crazy about. These comments eventually led to a heated, but fortunately nonviolent, confrontation between the normally docile pitcher and Buster. The argument did, however, cause Tiny's pitching to become wild. Some pitches were now being hurled over the fence, endangering an older man and his grandchildren who were sitting in front of the family home across the street, directly in the line of fire. At this point, Grandpa started telling the agitated pitcher a thing or two about how it felt to be seated in front of one's own home on a quiet summer evening and be subjected to the equivalent of artillery fire. He even issued an ultimatum: "Next time the ball comes over the fence, you won't get it back!" Ho boy! Now there were at least three angry people.

My friends and I sensed the inevitability of a showdown of some sort. It didn't take long to materialize, as Tiny let go of a pitch that was so high that even the Jolly Green Giant equipped with stilts couldn't have touched it. Then the fireworks began in earnest, as the harried grandfather grabbed the ball as it bounced around on his doorstep, and declared that Tiny had seen the last of that baseball. Ho boy, again! That's all the angry pitcher had to hear.

Intent on getting back the ball, he immediately headed toward Grandpa, resembling a giraffe as his long legs carried him swiftly across the street. I can still hear Tiny's baseball cleats click, click, clicking as they made contact with the pavement.

I don't believe that the old man had expected this much of a reaction. Quickly coming to the conclusion that to retreat would be the most logical maneuver, he ran, baseball in hand, into his house via the side entrance, with Tiny only a few steps behind. Grandpa then got the surprise of his life when Tiny pulled the door open and started to enter the house. He got no farther than the threshold, as Grandpa, using a bottle of Clorox, belted Tiny squarely on the noggin, dropping him on the spot.

Of course we kids had followed the action not only with our eyes, but also with our quickly moving feet, reaching the doorway just as the bottle came crashing down on poor Tiny's head. Incredibly, there was a doctor's office merely a few feet from where Tiny was lying in a daze. Opening his door to find out what all the commotion was about, the first thing the doctor noticed was the sight of a bloody patient sprawled out almost on his doorstep.

Luckily this nasty incident ended with no permanent damage to anyone involved. But no doubt, those present would never forget it.

The "Year of the Acapulco Dive" was so filled with firsts, I fairly bubble with enthusiasm as I reminisce over them. To begin with, thanks to Mariano Fallorina, the area around my desk had the distinct fragrance of gardenias. This beautiful kid had developed the highly pleasing habit of bringing to class a single gardenia and placing it on my desk ... with nary a word. As soon as this lovely flower lost its scent, sure enough Mariano would replace it with a fresh one. He became our self-appointed class florist. I'd been accustomed to the traditional apple for the teacher, even receiving as much as a huge box of them one year for Christmas. But gardenias—and on a regular basis? How neat! How original!

Then there was the cute custom of my students handing in test papers which contained not only answers, but also little messages or jokes—for example: Why did the moron throw his wristwatch out the window? Answer: Because he wanted to see time fly! Mr. Sorgi, your baseball cap looks so old that it must have belonged to Babe Ruth ... when he was a kid!

Often these remarks were accompanied by drawings. What the heck! I was always writing all sorts of comments on their corrected test papers: Jazzy! Neato! Whizzo! Oops! You're lookin' great, Johnny! Marvey, Joanna! Why shouldn't they be allowed to express themselves? I loved this means of communication and knew the kids also greatly enjoyed it, especially those who found it easier to express themselves in this manner rather than verbally.

To be sure, kids love class parties—understatement of understatements! Well, that year, in addition to the usual parties at Halloween, Christmas, Easter, and Valentine's Day, each student got to have a quickie five-minute party on his birthday. It was a simple, little thing ... a cupcake with one candle would be put on the Birthday Kid's desk as the class and I sang "Happy Birthday." Those five-minute parties were also provided for those whose birthdays didn't happen to fall on school days. Going one step further, even children unfortunate enough to have summer birthdays weren't left out. A little party was held for this small group, too. That satisfied everyone, made "Happy Birthday" number one on that year's hit parade, and kept my wife busy baking.

While on the topic of parties, the kids gave me one that year that deserved some kind of special award. Oh, did they do it up right!

Most surprisingly, it had the important element of surprise—I mean *real* surprise. In past years I was almost always able to sense when the kids were going to throw a "surprise" party for me. It was then essential for me to play dumb, as they went about making their supposedly secret plans, which lacked even the basic rudiments of secrecy. Long in advance, I'd know I shouldn't expect to get a full day's work done on May 12th, my birthday.

On this occasion, though, the kids set the party up in such a manner that even the administration and office staff were in on it to help make it truly an event to remember. So that they could have the time necessary to spring the shindig on me in a most dramatic manner, the kids had Duane Crawford, the principal, summon me to the office. Was I baffled! When I got there, Duane started asking me an assortment of silly questions, while trying hard to act serious. I couldn't help wondering just exactly what was going on. When the principal found it too awkward to continue asking me inane questions, he suggested that we go to my room.

The transformation that had taken place in my classroom while Duane performed his commendable stalling act was nothing short of amazing. The atmosphere was most definitely festive.

As we entered the room, the class sang "Happy Birthday" loud enough for the whole town of Freedom to hear. One of the children's mothers had baked a gorgeous cake fit for royalty and topped it with at least a dozen pieces of my favorite confection, marzipan fruits. All I could do was sit in my chair overwhelmed with feelings of love for these very special children. What a wonderful surprise! How thoughtful of my class to do things up so perfectly.

Two months earlier these children had given me an Award of Recognition on which was printed the following: This certificate is awarded to Mr. Robert Sorgi, Our Favorite Teacher, at Freedom, California, this 19th day of March, 1965. Each member of the class had signed the award. I was being killed with kindness. As Maxwell Smart would say: and loving it!

As a finale on the subject of parties that year, on the night before Valentine's Day, I decided to make my own valentines for the kids and hastily composed little rhymes to write on these cards ... you know, the personal touch. I used white art paper and a red pencil to draw the simplest of designs: hearts, arrows, that sort of thing. And then I quickly added such silly little ditties as: Love, kisses, things like that, Happy Valentine's Day, ya nice, little brat! Love ya madly! Even sillier was one that went like this: Gorgeous, fantastic, whizzo, swell ... everybody loves you, even the farmer in the dell! And here's, perhaps, the silliest: Nine times zero equals zero, this I'm sure you know ... but are you aware that to me you are truly whizzo? (As a background to this venture into poetry at its corniest, I heard, not watched, a Kathryn Grayson–Mario Lanza movie on the Extremely Late Show. The music was wonderful.)

The next day, I placed the personalized valentines on the children's desks before they got to the room. When they entered and went to their desks, the looks of surprise and delight on their faces more than compensated me for the mental exertion of having composed the corny lines in the wee hours of the morning.

I'm sitting at the beach in Carmel, California. Besides being awestruck by the sheer beauty of a seascape second to none, I'm reminiscing about a field trip on a spring day nineteen years ago, perhaps to the very day. In my mind's eye, I see Wayne Parker. He's gleefully running and sliding along the wet sand at the edge of the surf on a thin piece of wood known as skeetboard. Wow, this sure beats school, his eyes seem to say. Other members of my class are frolicking on the beach at water's edge. Some kids, their appetites stimulated by the sea air, have already started munching on sandwiches and swigging soft drinks.

There's a kite flying over the town of Carmel. It's quite high, but for the life of me, I can't figure out why it doesn't seem to go any higher even though I let out more and more string. The kite just hangs there, like an aerial buoy, its string now sagging ridiculously in the shape of a crescent moon. Somebody's giving me advice on how to fly a kite. Lo and behold, it's Sue. That suits me fine. I love having her along. (Too bad she didn't supply me with instructions each time she told me to "go fly a kite." If she had, I'd

probably be doing a better job now.) Well ... I'll be ...
even our two little tykes are here! And just to make sure
they're looked after *properly*, none other than my mother-in-
law *and* father-in-law have made themselves available. Just
a second ... Sue is now making threats and unhappy sounds
in the direction of a dog who is attempting to befriend our
daughters. I tell her to cool it. She responds with, "Haven't
you heard of mother's instinct?" My answer: "Certainly ...
but has the poor dog?"

Each year in early spring, my class would get to go on a
field trip to world-famous Carmel, within an hour's drive of
Freedom. It was, unquestionably, the event of the year for
the kids. From the opening day of school, I'd start telling
them all about the fabulous places to be enjoyed in Carmel,
not to mention the opportunity of wading around in the
water—all of this on a school day, no less! It may have been
called a field trip but, in reality, it was more in the way of an
educational picnic, with emphasis on both *educational* and
picnic.

The trip always took place in the latter part of the school
year after I'd had ample time to familiarize my class with
behavior that would be apt to leave people smiling instead
of growling and muttering nastily. Upon boarding the bus
and heading for our one-day stand in "paradise," I could
simply relax, enjoy the scenic ride and trust that my class
would leave the lovely village in the same condition in which
they'd find it.

There was a set of rules that left little or nothing to
the imagination: The school bus will be parked on Ocean
Avenue right by the beach. It returns to Freedom at one
o'clock. Be on it no later than 12:50 P.M. Throw absolutely
nothing on the ground, unless your stomach leaves you little
choice. In which case, do try to pick a spot that will cause
minimal offense. Make frequent use of words such as *Please,
Thank you, You're welcome, Pardon me,* and *Sorry.* When

entering places of business, keep your voices down. Restrict your screaming and hollering to the beach. Do not go into the water much beyond your ankles.

That was it ... all the rules that would make it a smooth, fun-filled day. The only place where I kept a close watch on the class was at the beach, which was the first spot we visited and the only time during our tour of Carmel when we were all together. Once we left the beach, the kids were on their own and they knew it. I trusted them as much as it was possible to trust any kids, and not once did they let me down over the years.

There was no way for me to keep close tabs on almost three dozen children scattered all over town. But their behavior must have been exemplary. Shopkeepers don't make a practice of giving gifts to rowdy kids. I mentioned earlier the generosity of a bookseller in giving one of my students a gift book. Well, the place was Carmel.

On another occasion, two beautifully carved gourds from South America were given to me by the owner of the Peruvian Shop as I browsed around the place with members of my class. I was speechless ... which for me was quite a feat! These gourds eventually went to the lucky winners of a drawing held in class a few days after the trip.

The first field trip I ever took a class on was to a candy factory, an ideal place for kids to visit, especially since they all received samples of the candy they had watched being made. But in Carmel it was a case of many field trips rolled up into one, as we casually toured numerous places where craftsmen were at work creating articles of distinction, and visited shops where a variety of unusual products were sold.

Foremost in my mind is the glassblower's shop located in a little arcade, just off Ocean Avenue, Carmel's main street. With each visit, he could be found immersed in his delicate world of glass, creating articles of great beauty with a facility gained by years and years of practice. This gentleman was only too glad to answer our questions in detail, which meant he had to stop working, because blowing glass and talking at the same time was hardly possible. I can still see him custom crafting a most fragile sailing ship for one of the kids, who was then obliged to spend the rest of the day looking like a human cage, both arms wrapped around the box containing his treasure, saying, "Watch it! Don't get too close. I want this thing to get home in one piece." Dave Middleton, you looked great that day ... a little overly protective but great nonetheless! Where are you now?

Back to the Peruvian Shop. It's best for a teacher to plan field trips that tie in with topics being studied by his class. Right? Definitely! This charming shop with its vast array of colorful wares originating in Latin America was "it" as far as I was concerned. Having heard so much about wool from the alpaca and vicuña, and places such as Bolivia and Argentina, it was reassuring to the kids to see sweaters with labels reading, Genuine alpaca—Made in Bolivia, or Made in Argentina—100% vicuña. It was thrilling to hear "Mr. Sorgi, look at this hat. Says here that it was made in Ecuador. Ooh, here's coffee from Costa Rica. How neat! Hey, does anybody know what *Hecho en Mexico* means?"

This was the type of dialogue I was interested in and the Peruvian Shop was just the place to stimulate it. Now the knowledge that the children had been accumulating was much more meaningful than before. Which reminds me, when I saw my first cow being milked, it was difficult for me to comprehend that the white liquid in the bucket was the same as that which came in a milk bottle. Being a wee lad from the northernmost reaches of The Bronx where farms had gone the way of the dodo bird, I hadn't been privileged to see such sights before and was, therefore, in a state of wonderment upon seeing milk actually coming out of a cow.

To stop at Carmel's De Smet Bakery Shop for some marzipan was always a must. Ah, marzipan! I believe that if any food deserves to be called "food for the gods," this delectable treat for the palate made from almond paste merits the title.

During the Christmas season, my father would bring home, among a vast assortment of goodies, this heavenly confection. My salivary glands are working double time as I remember the pretty candies in the shapes and colors of various fruits—oranges, pears, strawberries, apples—wrapped in cellophane and hanging temptingly on our Christmas tree. Pop bought these delicious holiday treats at a German delicatessen.

Just to make sure his family wouldn't have to wait until next Christmas to again partake of this incredible edible, at Eastertime my father never failed to buy a paschal lamb made of marzipan at an Italian pastry shop. This lamb was about six or seven inches long, approximately three inches wide and roughly three inches high, and had a tiny Italian flag stuck in it. To guarantee that it would last longer than the marzipan fruits that were picked off the Christmas tree with abandon, the cute little lamb was kept in the china closet, in plain view, but protected from instant consumption by a lock. Mom was the keeper of the key. Given this sort of sanctuary, the lamb lasted quite a while, although it did become something less than lovely as small chunks of its anatomy were cut off and eaten. In the end, all that was left was the little Italian flag.

During the Easter season, attention had been focused on the china closet. But once the paschal lamb was gone, this attractive piece of furniture was no longer in the limelight.

Long before going on our Carmel trip, the children had heard much about marzipan, but practically none of them had ever tasted it. This unfortunate state of affairs was easily remedied by a visit to the aforementioned bakery—De Smet's—which produces a quality of marzipan ranking with the best. But you know something? After tasting it, a few of the kids made funny faces, thus indicating to me, with as much tact as eleven- and twelve-year-olds are capable of, that they preferred less exotic sweets such as chocolate, jawbreakers, or just plain bubble gum, for that matter! My response was that maybe if they ate enough marzipan, they would eventually acquire a taste for it. Their answer was the equivalent of Why bother? ... as they gladly donated to me whatever marzipan they'd purchased. Happily, many of the kids thought it tasted great. So my marzipan promotional campaign was a success after all.

Art galleries, shops specializing in candles, leather goods, fine American Indian jewelry ... you name it ... we saw it. When the children noticed the price tags on some of the artwork in the galleries, they forgot to close their mouths. So I proceeded to explain to them that artists who could command such prices were few and far between. But they still found it difficult to comprehend a price of two thousand dollars ... for *any* work of art!

Ever hear of an Indian named Old Gabriel? This native Californian from the central coast supposedly breathed his last after having trod the earth for a grand total of 151 years! You may find that hard to believe. So did a long-forgotten engraver. In the Carmel Mission cemetery, where Old Gabriel is resting, the age engraved on his tombstone is 119. This age is certainly more realistic.

Carmel—what a place for a field trip! With so much to see, 12:50 P.M., our bus-boarding time, always came much too soon. Yet, I can't remember ever having to wait for anyone. From hither, thither and yon, all of us would have boarded the bus by one o'clock and been on our way back to Freedom School ... happily exhausted.

Prior to arriving at the beach today, a little walking and talking revealed to me that a few of our favorite places are no more. The Peruvian Shop is gone. The glassblower died a short while ago. Where he created beautiful objects of glass, an imaginative fellow named Claude Kremer works with a collection of stamps and coins in fashioning highly unusual gifts. The Robert John Leather Shop where, on one of our field trips, I bought Sue a suede coat with a mink collar, no longer exists. But all is not lost. For the De Smet Bakery, to which my feet automatically gravitated, is still doing a brisk business and its marzipan is still just as good as it ever was.

In between the lighthearted activities that were so much a part of the year, I was very pleased with what happened academically, especially in math. Two years before, it had been such a struggle for my class to achieve an average of 80 percent on math tests. Since then, however, the 90 percent barrier had been broken in math, leaving me to wonder if there was any limit to what children could accomplish. From all indications, this breakthrough wasn't attributable to greater brainpower but to more concentration on the basics, particularly the multiplication tables, and to a sustained emphasis on motivation. Once an entire class had virtually mastered the tables up to and including the 9s, multiplying became a snap, and division, even with its many steps, couldn't help being easier.

Just think of how much motivation is needed to produce championship teams in sports. My attitude was: Why not motivate for math tests as if a championship were at stake each time? I felt that for a heterogeneous class, with its wide range of IQs, a 90 percent average would be truly an accomplishment of championship caliber. (No, we didn't have math rallies with cheerleaders chanting: Hey, hey, whaddya say ... avoid teacher's wrath, break 90 in math!)

There was a practice session before each math test, with much attention being given to those who needed it most. Time and time again, my students were told to check each example after it was done, or after the test was completed. And yet simple mistakes went undetected.

One day, though, while hitting on all mental cylinders, I came up with an idea for checking math work that really produced results. It won't get me asked to the Institute of Advanced Studies at Princeton, but when compared to conventional methods of checking examples, it was different, albeit somewhat time-consuming. Here's the procedure that was used:

Each student took the test twice, using two separate pieces of paper. The papers weren't to be compared until both had been completed. Then, if after comparing the two papers, all the answers matched, the chances were excellent that the student's grade was 100 percent. Either paper could be turned in. Now let's suppose that when comparing papers, there were two different answers for example number five. No big deal. This example would have to be done over as many times as it took to get the same answer twice. Of course, if many answers didn't match, the conclusion was that the test had been done carelessly. Eventually, it didn't take this lengthy procedure for the kids to average 90 percent and better. But I believe it had served its purpose well.

The summer that followed this great year was one of my busiest ever. Besides teaching summer school, tutoring an adult in basic reading skills and an eighth grader in general studies, I even did a stint as a film evaluator. In spite of all these activities, my family and I managed to squeeze in a two-week vacation in the boonies of interior British Columbia.

Sue and I decided that Anne, at two years of age, could handle the wilderness trek that had been planned. Veronica, at eight months, was deemed a bit young for a trip that would eventually total more than three thousand miles. Her grandparents in Salinas made sure, however, that Ronnie was babysat properly ... and spoiled adequately.

Having room to spare, we invited my mom and Aunt Mary to come along. With my father, New York City's walking Chamber of Commerce, constantly complaining that living in the city of Santa Cruz was tantamount to being in solitary confinement, the thought of asking him to come on a vacation that would place him in the midst of a frontier setting was too funny for words.

The trip was perfectly relaxing until we started heading west after reaching Williams Lake, British Columbia. Our final destination was a remote guest ranch at Mons Lake, approximately ninety miles away. According to a service station attendant at Williams Lake, it might take as much as five hours to reach the ranch. This had sounded ultraconservative and we wondered how the road could be in such bad repair as to require traveling at an average speed of less than twenty miles per hour. The road map hadn't indicated that any unusual road conditions existed.

It took only a few miles of travel on that road to realize that even ten miles per hour would be a chancy speed in many places. Rocky and dusty, this extremely rugged route resembled a washboard, with enough sharp curves and narrow spots to keep me very apprehensive ... and extra careful. I'm sure all of us expected to meet our Maker at any moment. All of us, that is, except Annie. To her, this primitive road was a special treat with all its bumps, turns, funny sounds, and dirt flying around all over the place. She probably figured that Daddy was playing some sort of game just for her amusement and responded with shrieks of wild laughter so typical of children unable to contain their joy. The worse the road became, the more Annie laughed! Still, she must have been curious as to why nobody else was laughing. All I could think of was how right that guy at the service station had been. We'd started at five o'clock in the afternoon and, at this point, would have been delighted to be sure of arriving at Mons Lake by ten.

About midway in our journey, at a very narrow section of the road, what should we encounter but a barely moving car filled with inordinately happy people. As I passed the car at about two miles per hour, we heard the driver offer us some beer. I couldn't imagine anything that we needed less! Farther down the road was a small encampment of Indians living in wigwams, yet. What an incongruity in the jet age!

As we continued to make our way along this rugged road with a 1962 Rambler that was designed for much less adventurous driving, we all must have been thinking: So far, so good. And then it happened!

What could be worse than coming to a fork in the road with no signs, when you're in the middle of nowhere? I'll tell you what: taking the wrong road in the fork ... which is most likely to occur, if Murphy's Law has any validity. You expect the odds of taking the wrong road to be fifty-fifty, but somehow they "ain't." While on the subject of odds ... why is it that when a ground ball takes a bad hop, it's always on the *last* hop, just as you're about to field it? Be that as it may ... coming to the fork in the road and not having a clue as to which road to take, I chose the one on the left. It immediately proved to be a very wet, gooey cow pasture with numerous bovines observing us curiously, a look in their eyes appearing to say: No way! Fearful of becoming hopelessly mired down in this no-man's-land, I steered the car ever so gingerly out of that pasture and headed for the other fork in the road.

On reaching it, I found that it was deeply rutted and full of good-sized rocks and branches. Obviously it would be impossible to drive past that mess. My Aunt Mary was now of the opinion that she should go off on her own to inspect the area on foot, making like a modern pathfinder. The word she used was *reconnoiter*. When we all looked at her cross-eyed, she apparently dismissed the idea from her mind on the double.

When I'd hauled off the largest rocks and branches barring the way and emptied the car of its passengers, I was able to drive through this deeply gouged section of road, the loud grinding and scraping doing nothing positive for our already mangled nerves. Again, Annie thought this to be another act in a continuing comedy designed for her pleasure, and laughed her head off!

Believe it or not, all of this strenuous activity proved to be totally unnecessary because the road led back to the soggy cow pasture ... which had been the right road to begin with!

Sure enough, close to five hours after leaving Williams Lake, we arrived at the ranch. I'd written to the owners, Ron and Mary Nelson, a few weeks earlier but hadn't made any definite reservations. Therefore when I tapped on their door so unexpectedly, explaining who I was and pointing to a car full of people ranging in age from two to seventy-three, their mouths suddenly opened and emitted what sounded like muffled gasps! I believe their temporary dumbfoundedness was caused by the thought of what an awful situation it could have been, if they had been booked solid.

With a show of hospitality and a look of amused puzzlement, they cordially invited us into their home, and fed and entertained us as if we'd been old friends. When evening shadows fell and we and the Nelsons sat conversing in the dark, it was our turn to be amusedly puzzled. Were these wonderful folks night people, able to see without benefit of lights?

Phrasing my question as delicately as possible, I finally decided to ask about the absence of lights. The answer was simple and the first in a series of surprises we were in for that evening. The darkness was due to the fact that the Nelsons generated their own electricity and used it sparingly. No lights had been turned on because talking was just as easy without them. They did offer to light kerosene lanterns if we wished. That was the source of light for the cabins, we were told.

Our disappointment was evident but we couldn't very well say Sorry folks, we didn't plan to rough it this much. ... How much do we owe you for the food? We're heading back to Williams Lake. So we laughed it off and said the equivalent of No sweat.

The "best" surprise came next. On the way to our cabin we were informed that the outhouse was only a short walk away ... in the woods. Now, for some of us, nature was calling loud and clear. The last thing we felt like doing was stumbling around in the woods in search of an outhouse, especially because we'd been expecting modern conveniences at the end of our grueling drive.

No sooner had Mary Nelson mentioned the word *outhouse* than Mom, Aunt Mary, Sue, and I began to laugh just about as hard as was humanly possible. Oh how good it felt, to hear all that laughter! I'm sure Annie didn't know why we were laughing but she added her laughter to ours. It was easy to see that Mrs. Nelson understood the meaning of all this laughter. In such a predicament, it was either laugh or sulk. Spontaneously, we had chosen to laugh, trying to make the best of the situation.

Actually, the inconveniences were soon forgotten, and a great vacation was had by all in a setting of wilderness splendor. Having dreamt for years of finding a fishing Shangri-la where fish could be caught by the dozen, my dream had become a reality. The only trouble was, I hooked so many rainbows that fishing at Mons Lake eventually bored me. Unbelievable!

As we left for home, the Nelsons thanked us for being "such good sports." I could hardly wait to tell the story of this trip when I got back to my natural habitat ... a classroom full of kids!

Chapter Nine

How Many People in Katmandu Have Asthma

"Mr. Sorgi, we see so many films that our room might as well be named Studio 11, instead of Room 11!" This was the general consensus of my thirty-four sixth grade students early in the 1965–66 school year.

I'd always been reluctant to show films. My unwillingness was due, basically, to a lack of confidence in projectors. As a student, I had sat back many a time watching a teacher or group of teachers trying with all their might to make a projector do what it was intended to do. Success was usually achieved only after much fiddling around, with the classroom lights being turned off and on repeatedly.

During the past summer I was one of several teachers paid by the Santa Cruz County Office of Education to view films. The object was to judge which films in its library should be declared obsolete and eliminated, and which newly produced films should be purchased. Me, of all people, being a determining factor in the selection of films!

One guess as to what those viewing sessions did for me. You've got it! They made me a believer—anxious not only to show films to my class, but also to promote their use. The only trouble was, I hadn't learned how to use a film projector. Because I love to laugh, even if it's at myself, I really wish that first attempt of mine at using a film projector could have been filmed. So help me, it seemed that everything that should not have happened did, in fact, happen!

One morning I decided my kids should no longer be denied the pleasant and efficient means of learning afforded by films. (If a picture is worth a thousand words, how many words is a film worth?) A fellow teacher on the other wing had a good film that she was only too glad to let me use. When it became known to her that my ignorance in the use of projectors was complete, she pointed to the directions clearly shown on the projector. To be really nice, she set up the film for me so that it was ready to be shown. All I'd have to do would be to turn on the projector.

"Great! Thank you, ma'am," I said, as I headed back hastily and jubilantly to my students. The occasion was a prime example of haste making waste.

The projector was on a cart. As I wheeled it along, everything went fine until its front wheels hit a small bump. (If only the next few scenes could have been filmed!) Well, the first thing that happened was this: The front reel containing the film hadn't been fully secured to the projector and therefore decided to fall off. It started rolling away from me, down the sidewalk, all the while letting out many, many feet of film. In a panic, I began chasing the reel but then noticed it wasn't the only thing that had started to travel. The cart containing the projector was now slowly on its way to wherever!

A decision had to be made very quickly as to which needed pursuing more: the reel, rolling merrily along as its film unwound, or the projector, which hadn't yet gone very far. I chose the reel. Grabbing the thing firmly while keeping an eye on the projector which, happily, had stopped moving, I now started gathering up the film. Of course, it was twisted up but good, and naturally, the wind was blowing to beat the band. Just to complicate matters even further, the film had broken. All I could think was: I've just mutilated a beautiful and expensive film. What a total idiot I am!

All of this happened with nobody in sight to give me a hand. By the time I untwisted the film, rewound it back on the reel, attached the reel to the projector, and reached my room, I was spent. It was as if I'd done a full day's work. Yet, it was only mid-morning.

Too flustered to try to figure out how to remove the broken section of film which remained in the projector, I finally sought help. But not before the reel had once again found its way to the ground. In this manner was Studio 11 founded!

Very early I discovered dozens of sources from which films could be borrowed ... free. The most logical place to start was the Santa Cruz County Office of Education, from which films could be obtained almost immediately. Because our film-viewing team had spent so many hours watching films—chief film man Donn Wallace claimed our eyeballs were becoming rectangular in shape—I was well-acquainted with the office's film library. Two films that really impressed my students and me were *Grand Canyon* and *Pablo—Boy of Mexico.*

Grand Canyon was a newly purchased silent film that told its story through use of the latest techniques in photography and the music of Ferde Grofè's "Grand Canyon Suite." The actors and actresses consist solely of wildlife. How unforgettable is the sidewinder rattlesnake, laboriously making its way up a sand hill, illustrating the point that if at first you don't succeed, try, try again!

This film definitely captures some of the canyon's most dramatic moods during all four seasons. There's rain, snow, thunder, lightning, wind, and, most impressive of all, the multiple shades of light produced by the almost unreal cloud formations.

Before describing *Pablo—Boy of Mexico,* I'd like to refer to a film I saw in 1961. Until then, I wasn't able to understand how any movie could so affect a person as to cause tears to be shed in so public a place as a theater. I mean there is such a thing as self-control, stiff upper lip ... that sort of thing. That's what I'd thought. And then it very nearly happened to me, much to my surprise. The name of the movie escapes me but its beginning was absolutely heartrending.

A car is shown traveling along a country road. Its occupants are a jovial family whom I'll call the Hansens— Mr. and Mrs. Hansen, their son, about twelve years of age, and a German shepherd. Suddenly, and I mean *very* suddenly, another car appears, seemingly from out of nowhere, forcing the Hansens' car off the road. The car overturns, coming to rest in a fairly concealed spot, as the other driver continues on his way at a high rate of speed. The result: both parents are killed, the boy sustains a serious head injury, and the dog runs from the scene of the accident in search of help for his family.

Eventually the boy is rescued and recovers ... but only after being reunited with his faithful dog, following a lengthy search. To me it was as if this horrid accident had actually occurred. I wanted so much to cry ... to take that boy in my arms and hug him ever so tightly. But all I could do was get an immense lump in my throat and try with all my might to suppress any tears, lest people in the audience stare at me. Somehow I succeeded in holding back the tears, like a "manly" twenty-eight-year-old.

Pablo—Boy of Mexico was another film that touched me deeply. Pablo is a hardworking nine-year-old from a dirt-poor family. He helps his father in the fields and is thoughtful and considerate beyond his years. Pablo has one great desire ... to own a pair of new, black shoes, just like the ones he sees whenever he goes to the marketplace. He has never had shoes, and is trying to earn enough money to buy his dream shoes in time to wear them to the great religious celebration held each year in a nearby city. Oh, how the boy longs for that little pair of black shoes! He's constantly aware of how much more money is needed in order to make them his.

One day, however, Pablo's baby sister becomes alarmingly ill. With little money available for medical bills, the family's money supply is quickly depleted and the boy, without being asked, contributes his hard-earned cash, fervently hoping it will help his little sister to recuperate. The baby does get well and Pablo resigns himself to going to the great celebration in sandals, as usual.

Well, the big day comes and the family attends the *fiesta,* walking all the way to the city. Pablo wonders whatever became of the fancy *sombrero* his father always wears to the fiesta. He doesn't have long to wonder as Papa presents his beautiful child with the brand-new, shiny pair of black shoes the boy had so fervently desired, yet had been willing to sacrifice for the sake of his baby sister. Pablo now understands why his father no longer has his fancy sombrero and where the money to buy his new, shiny black shoes has come from.

By the time the film was over, ho boy, was I in trouble ... my eyes ready to pour out a veritable stream of tears. But again, I managed to stifle the likes of tears ... until a time two years hence, when holding them back would become too herculean a task for me.

At the conclusion of each film, there'd be a question-and-answer period. Whenever correct answers were given, they were written on the board. The kids could then see how the words they'd been hearing in the film were spelled, a definite aid, I believe, in the acquisition and retention of knowledge.

Very quickly I became a prime advocate of audiovisual education. Too bad it hadn't occurred sooner.

In addition to the county, I discovered dozens of other sources from which films could be obtained free of charge, such as Kodak, Ford Motor Company, Texaco, the American and National baseball leagues, and the local library. When my Acapulco Kids from the previous year found out about my film-showing binges, their noses were a little out of joint. They decried the fact that I hadn't adopted this beautiful method of teaching just one year sooner.

To sort of rectify this situation, I agreed to show films to them after school. Quite a few took me up on my offer and made the short trek from Rolling Hills Junior High School to Room 11, to see what they could see.

With all this practice in the use of film projectors, I developed an impressive facility in their use, even coolly coping with the occasional, yet very frustrating, breakdowns. (Incidentally, the true test of whether a teacher's a real pro comes when a projector makes up its mind to malfunction, with a huge audience of squirmy kids practicing the vice, or art, of impatience. The trick is to convince the projector to serve its intended purpose quickly, without further ado. It isn't cool to allow the noise from the restless audience to reach such a crescendo as to necessitate an emotional display terminating with such words as *shut up!*)

Actually, my adventures into the realm of audiovisual education had begun the previous year with the introduction of Music Appreciation. Music has always been a most important part of my life. It's hard for me to picture being home or at the drugstore (my second home) without the sound of music as an integral part of the environment. (For all I know, the Sorgi family may even have inspired background music!)

At the drugstore it was classical music *all the time!* I mean constantly! Just imagine Carnegie Hall with a pharmaceutical decor and aroma, and you've got the picture.

This setting attracted a number of music *aficionados* with impressive backgrounds in music. In time there developed a musical fraternity of sorts. The leader of this group, of necessity, was Professor Carl Hauser, a noted musician who'd been well acquainted with one of symphonic music's giants, Johannes Brahms. Imagine what a thrill it was for my father, who idolized Brahms to such a degree that he wrote a book about him, to count Professor Hauser among his friends! Good grief, my father could say that he shook the hand that shook the hand of Johannes Brahms, one of the world's greatest composers! Professor Hauser was a beautifully gentle man, who always had a twinkle in his eye. With the addition of about fifty pounds, he would have looked like the perfect Santa Claus.

Not included among the classical music buffs, but unforgettable nonetheless, were the brothers Sid and Sam Spielburg. They could not rightfully belong because they dug swing too much, at a time when liking swing was, to many classical music lovers, equal to musical heresy. Oh, yeah, swing was considered quite anathema.

But how could anyone ever forget two guys who'd come, literally, bouncing into the drugstore, most of the time unexpectedly, and start harmonizing loudly, no matter who was present? One would sing while the other played an imaginary bass. Pity those customers present who were unfamiliar with the antics of these two wild, one-of-a-kind characters!

Sid dabbled in songwriting. He wrote a tune called "Stormy Crossing," which he claimed we would hear if only we'd listen to a *certain* radio station, at a *certain* time, on a *certain* day. Either our signals got crossed, or our collective hearing paraphernalia wasn't working properly, because none of us, listening with bated breath, ever did hear that tune. Is it possible that, as their zany business card proclaimed, they were "Rejected by the Best"?

At home, classical music reigned supreme every morning until around nine o'clock. By then my father was on his way to work and my mother welcomed the opportunity of enjoying some silence. How strange ordinary sounds seemed when not heard in concert with music!

Visiting our home between 5:30 and 7:30 on any evening meant one thing for sure: Martin Block and his famous "Make Believe Ballroom." With both my parents at the drugstore, swing was king.

Martin Block. Find a swing enthusiast who lived during the swing era, yet never heard of Martin Block, and you'll more than likely be in the presence of someone from outer space. Such was this man's popularity, and, I believe, justifiably so.

Block was the epitome of sophistication, with a liberal sprinkling of warmth, which, to his listeners, was a tough combination to beat. I've often wondered just how much of swing's popularity was due to his promoting it. He was, undoubtedly, one of the world's first disc jockeys and in this role couldn't have better represented the music industry.

Block's famous program, "The Make Believe Ballroom," came on in both the morning and evening. Each evening in our home, on WNEW radio, immediately following the 5:30 news, you could hear the show's theme song, "It's Make Believe Ballroom Time," played by the Glenn Miller Band. This signalled the start of two hours of swing music, divided into fifteen-minute segments, each featuring a different big band, small group, or vocalist.

I'd say the show's highlight of the year was a contest to determine the top bands. Oh, how I looked forward to the evening when the names of the most popular big bands were announced. Seems to me that Glenn Miller was usually the top banana.

Particularly heartwarming was his Christmas Eve program when Block described, in minute detail, Christmas cards sent to him by the musical artists whom he'd helped to make famous.

Let's assume that when good deejays die, they go to that "big radio station in the sky," in which case, Martin Block (often referred to, by me, as a member of the family) has, for almost twenty years, been proudly spinning such tunes as Jimmy Dorsey's "The Breeze And I," Glenn Miller's "String Of Pearls," Bobby Sherwood's "Elk's Parade," and a multitude of other swinglike sounds he relished so much.

Whatever expertise it takes to listen to and appreciate music, I firmly believe it would be safe to say that I have achieved same. Very early, I came to love music in general, and classical, swing, and jazz in particular. As a child, my listening wasn't restricted to radio. We were owners (proud or otherwise) of a tiny phonograph so primitive that today it would be considered laughable. Compared to the wondrous sounds produced by the stereo systems of the 1980s, our itsy-bitsy, little phono was something out of The Flintstones. The needle actually required changing after only a few records had been played. No matter. That simple piece of electronic equipment was played for hours at a time. I listened to Wagner's "Ride of the Valkyrie" and Ponchielli's "Dance of the Hours" over and over. Then the tempo changed dramatically as tunes such as Charlie Barnet's "Cherokee," Glenn Miller's "Bugle Call Rag," and Artie Shaw's "Yesterdays" could be heard throughout the house.

In addition to listening to music, I also made some of my own, although I can't say it was exactly my idea. My mother was of the opinion that her son, Robert, should learn to play the piano, which, in fact, I did. This obligation was sometimes complicated to a great degree, by the dialogue emanating from 236th Street. It went something like this:

Throw the ball here, jerk, or Why don't you pitch it right? Are you blind or something? Then there might be the question asked when a stickball batter chose to wait too long for the right pitch: Whaddya want, egg in your beer? ... whatever *that* was supposed to mean!

At such times, I couldn't help wondering why I should ... indeed, how I could, learn to play "Ciribiribin" with so much stickball being played within earshot. Through sheer perseverance, magnified by an unquenchable desire to go out and play, I did learn to play "Ciribiribin" or a reasonable facsimile thereof well enough to perform it for a neighbor, who could have shown more enthusiasm.

As time went by, though, I drifted away from the piano. Mom must have tired of constantly having to coax and pressure me into practicing; so naturally, I took advantage of this situation. A quarter of a century later, I taught myself to play the piano. But never, not once, have I posed the slightest threat to any of the great pianists ... or even to the worst, for that matter.

The purpose of introducing the kids to classical music and other musical forms such as swing, jazz, and folk was to enable them to hear music that might become a source of great pleasure to them. It was clear that very few of the children had had much experience with the sounds they were hearing.

On many an afternoon, just after lunch, we'd all simply relax and listen to music. It was mostly of the classical variety, ranging from Beethoven to Gershwin. At the end of a listening session, I'd ask each student to grade the selections on a scale of A to F. All that was needed was a slip of paper with a grade for each selection. I made it plain that names were not required. Otherwise the kids might inflate the grades to please me, which wasn't the point.

To my surprise and total delight, the most common grade was A. When Ravel's *Bolero* was played, the class became almost ecstatic. Too bad Ravel himself couldn't have been present to witness the joy that his music produced that day. (Having been entombed almost thirty years before, his appearance would have been quite a spectacle!) The kids, apparently each one of them, wanted an encore badly.

Now anyone familiar with *Bolero* knows that it is barely audible at the beginning but slowly increases in loudness until, at its finale, one's eardrums are assaulted without mercy. So, for it to be possible for my long-suffering fellow teacher next door to conduct class without screaming at the top of his lungs, I chose, instead, Claude Debussy's *Afternoon of a Faun,* an entrancing piece of music with a soft, dreamlike quality. The contrast couldn't have been greater. Following the excitement of *Bolero,* I feared that such a quiet selection would be a letdown. Far from it. They loved it! The music's serenity appeared to soothe them after the emotional exhaustion they had experienced as a result of hearing *Bolero.*

With such an exciting response, I, happily, had no choice but to continue with Music Appreciation. Some of the kids were so proud of the grades they gave to this music that they included their names next to the A+'s, along with such comments as Fantastic, Terrific, Jazzy, etc. One or two of the kids were not so enthusiastic. Along with the accolades came the occasional nameless slip of paper with a big, fat F emblazoned on it. The remarks were equally uncomplimentary. A few that have stuck in my mind were, It stinks, Awful, I give it an F. Wow, an F, yet. I had asked for honesty and gotten it, by golly. Maybe a hardy dislike was more desirable than lukewarmness.

One thing was for certain. Between films and recordings, Room 11 was now fully audiovisualized and happily so. My, what a far cry from the classrooms I'd been accustomed to as a student.

Looking at thirty-four smiling (or at least not grumpy) faces surrounding a picture of Freedom School with its in-

famous, accordion-like roof, my thoughts run along these
lines: Where are these 31- or 32-year-olds now? With the
exception of two, I don't even have a clue, not a single, solitary clue as to their whereabouts. Just for starters, where is
Dennis Haskins? He displays one of the most self-confident
smiles ever captured by a camera. His expression seems to
say: Look at my beautiful, straight, and white teeth. Aren't
I a neat kid? Yes, Dennis, you certainly were just that!
But do you know what comes to mind when I think of you,
buddy? It was your singular love of music. How gratifying it
was to see you sitting there drinking it all in, note for note.

Recently, during a local jazz festival, I read in the newspaper the names of the participating musicians. The name
Haskins jumped up out of the page. It was, however, the
wrong Haskins. Wouldn't it have been a kick if it *had* been
the right Haskins? I would've looked around until I'd found
you. You can bet your boots on that!

The second person to the left of Dennis is Teddy Reyes.
His smile is a sort of male version of the Mona Lisa's. Teddy
was the quiet, unassuming type, a good, steady worker. As
a matter of fact, he was so quiet that it took me until the
latter part of the year to realize just how valuable an asset
he was to our class. But his classmates knew, all right.
I don't know how long it had taken *them* to realize it, but
when asked to vote for the person who was the best behaved,
hardest-working student in the class, their choice was the
same as mine ... Teddy Reyes!

Valerie is one of my favorite names. When the last name
accompanying it is Marquez, I fairly glow. This lovely girl
was the third member of the Marquez family that it was my
pleasure to teach. Valerie must have been born with the
smile she wears in this class picture.

All kids cry. (Isn't that a brilliant statement, requiring
great powers of observation!) Yet, trying to imagine Valerie

crying is not easy. I wonder how many kids with perpetual Valerie Marquez-like smiles call her "Mama"?

Back in the mid 1960s, the adjective, *trivial,* was heard now and then, just as it is today. On the other hand, the noun form, *trivia,* was lying in a dormant state, waiting to be provided with the impetus necessary to make it a household word. And who should make this possible? None other than the original "triviologist," the fourth person to the right of Valerie: Alan Iermini, whose brother, David, had done so much to enrich my class the previous year.

Alan had more bits and pieces of information floating around in his fertile mind than there are asteroids dancing about in the heavens. One day Alan left me speechless (not the easiest task) by mentioning the name, Nick Altrock, who'd played major league baseball years and years before. Now what's so unusual about that? you might ask. My answer would be, Nick Altrock, because of his clowning, was quite popular in his day. But even forty years ago his name wasn't likely to be heard, even on the lips of most baseball *cognoscenti,* let alone on those of an eleven-year-old. Oh, Big Al was knowledgeable, all right. I had to be on my toes whenever Alan was on one of his trivia sprees, which was daily and constantly.

Of that good crew of thirty-four, Alan is the only one I've actually seen in umpteen years. He still lives in the same house and works in Watsonville. If you ever wish to know, for example, how many people in Katmandu have asthma, or which of Yankee pitching great Red Ruffing's toes were cut off in an accident, just contact Alan Iermini, Watsonville, California. Should Al not know the answer, the information simply isn't available.

(This has nothing whatsoever to do with Alan or the class of 1965–66, but my state of happiness has just been increased immeasurably by the receipt of a letter and picture from a more recent champion of the past, Marcus Von Engel.

Again, how right was that speech professor of so long ago. Indeed, I *am* a millionaire!)

Chapter Ten

My Name Could Have Been Mud

"Boys and girls, would you please tell me what you see up against the wall to your left, at the back of the room? You say nothing? Well, you're correct, of course. There's nothing but empty space there now. Yet, within the next two months, that emptiness will no longer exist. In its place there will be a neat, little house with walls made of dried mud, topped with a roof of straw. And you kids will have built it. The house will even be large enough for one of you kids to sit in."

This was the manner in which I announced to my class, that as an art project connected with the study of Latin America, we'd be constructing a mud house, better known as an *adobe*. It was to be the first in a long line of far-out projects that my classes and I were to engage in over the coming years. Although appearing to be an excellent way to get a feel for life in Latin America, at least from the peasant's point of view, my planned project did sound rather wild, if I say so myself.

Show me a class that can dig up two yards of dirt, mix it with straw and water by kneading it barefooted, place this gooey mess into molds to form bricks, and then construct

a miniature adobe with these bricks, causing no damage to
life, limb, or property, and I'll show you a group of kids
with a unique sense of accomplishment ... and a very proud
teacher.

When I had first proposed this project to the principal,
Duane Crawford, a look of amazement and incredulity had
covered his normally placid face. Even more so when he was
told the idea was for this project to be completed within the
confines of the classroom and not outside. His eyes conveyed
the universal you've-got-to-be-kidding look I was to see so
often in future years.

Notwithstanding his look of disbelief, Duane's words were
something to the effect that I must know what I was doing. This man—as nice a guy as you could ever meet anywhere, by the way—probably wondered where I'd come up
with such a potentially disastrous art project, at a time
when most sixth graders were restricted to drawing paper,
crayons, paste, and scissors. (For the real adventurous
teacher—brave and fearless—there was always finger-
painting.)

The answer to that question was only two months in the
past. During the summer, I'd attended a six-week NDEA
Summer Institute on Latin American history, courtesy of
the United States government. The abbreviation stood for
National Defense Education Act, and I haven't the slightest
notion what a course in Latin American history had to do
with national defense. This course and many others were
offered in colleges throughout the United States. The government not only footed the tuition, but was so benevolent
as to support the teacher while he was being educated. If
said teacher happened to be married, his dependents, too,
were supported. What a sweet arrangement!

The only hitch was that, naturally, the competition for
these scholarships was keen. Well, I got lucky and was one
of thirty-five sixth grade teachers selected to study Latin

American history at the University of Santa Clara, only an hour's drive from home. I couldn't have been more thrilled at this turn of events.

What a fruitful summer it turned out to be. There was an enriching exchange of ideas among all the teachers, fine lectures, and lots of laughs, as well. One easygoing fellow teacher found the racetrack, and baseball at San Francisco's Candlestick Park, so enticing that his attendance at class was, perforce, limited to occasional "guest appearances" which could be, to say the least, quite colorful. At times, he'd sprawl out in a seat as if it were a recliner, and read the newspaper, mostly the sports pages—an image of total relaxation. A pipe and slippers would have put the finishing touches on this picture of contentment.

At the end of this course we were required to hand in a term paper. Mine was entitled "A Collection of Fascinating Facts About Latin America," which was designed to motivate children in such a way that they'd be anxious to learn about our neighbors to the south. Once more I was fortunate. What had been intended solely as a term paper was published, without my prior knowledge, in a national junior high school education publication.

Feeling especially creative that summer, I came up with an idea for an invention ... very surprising for one who leaves the operation of almost all complex mechanical contrivances to his more mechanically adept wife. Of all things, an automatic blackboard eraser seemed to be just what was needed. No more messy hands for this guy. All that was necessary was an electrically operated, three-foot-long eraser, with a windshield wiper–like motion, activated by merely turning on a switch. Presto, the board would be cleaned quickly by this quasi–Rube Goldberg–type mechanism. But, as we all realize, nothing is ever as easy as it looks. So I never did build a workable model, let alone get a patent, in spite

of my father's constant urging. I guess I just didn't want to
be bothered; eventually the scheme simply died on the vine.

This yearning for new and exciting ideas carried over into
the new school year. Hence, the adobe house project—to be
known, in time, as Adobe I ... to distinguish it from the
more "luxurious" later models.

If ever there were a case of self-discipline being an abso-
lute must, this was it. Everyone was told that whatever
mud was produced was meant to eventually become the
bricks that were to be used in constructing our adobe house.
Should any of the mud become airborne, the one or ones responsible for its having taken flight would be permanently
grounded from working on the project! With this warning
still ringing in their ears, they began working on this, if I
say so myself, daring endeavor.

In building an adobe house, logic dictates that the soil
used in making the bricks be of the adobe type. And that's
exactly the kind of soil we were fortunate enough to have on
the school grounds. Off in a remote corner of the property,
the dirt was first dug up. Then it was mixed with straw
and water so that this combination's consistency would be
just right. The next step was to fill wooden forms with the
gooey mess just produced. These forms were twelve inches
long, six inches wide, and four inches high. If too much water was added, the mud would lose its shape after the form
was removed. Too little water resulted in the mud's thick-
ness being such that it would stick to the form, producing
misshapen bricks.

The kids developed their brickmaking skills quickly. How
delighted they were in their work, especially while mixing the
mud and straw by kneading the gooey mess with their bare
feet. What a sight! If memory serves me correctly, poor
Duane didn't summon up the courage to view this daring
art project at its messiest stage.

During recesses, we drew quite a crowd with virtually the entire school very curious as to what on earth was happening. Our visitors had found it a bit much to believe that one class was actually getting to "play" in the mud. This incredible state of affairs had to be verified to be believed! Cleaning up before going into the cafeteria for lunch took some ingenuity. Not desiring to become a mortal enemy of the janitor as a result of mud-splattered rest rooms, the kids were obliged to divest themselves of large quantities of this offensive substance at the construction site. This was accomplished through the simple process of being hosed down by me with equally large quantities of water.

By the end of the day, upwards of 100 bricks had been made. There'd been no mud slinging, and a good and productive time had been had by all: The hardest phases of the job, however, were yet to come.

Adobe bricks need to be cured in the sun for best results, a process taking days of exposure to sunlight, out in the open. Would it be safe, though, to leave these tempting mudpies outside for that long a period of time? With ugly visions of vandals dancing in my head, I thought not.

The next morning I breathed a sigh of relief upon seeing that the bricks had remained undisturbed. Nevertheless, tempting fate was not my game. So that very same day, the kids and I brought the bricks into the classroom. Although we moved them prematurely, very few were damaged, even though they were far from being dry.

Conducting a class in a room with thirty children and nearly 100 wet mud bricks scattered hither, thither, and yon was *interesting*. It wasn't long, however, before this situation became totally untenable, what with all of us going through the motions of ballet artists to avoid stepping on the precious bricks.

What to do? Here's what. The decision was made to get the adobe house built immediately ... like next day. So help me, what followed should have been immortalized on film! Anyone visiting the school would have assumed that one of its classrooms was in the process of major alterations ... strange alterations, indeed, considering that kids could be seen hauling wheelbarrow loads of dirt into the classroom. I repeat ... this scenario should have been immortalized on film. Working as if there were the distinct possibility that there'd be no tomorrow, we put up the walls of our little house in a single day. That was the difficult part of the job because the roof was going to consist of nice, dry straw. Compared to working inside a classroom with so much damage possible, making the bricks out in a field had been a cinch.

Just as in any group, there were take-charge kids ... automatic foremen, so to speak. Two that come to mind instantly are Salvador Martin, a prince of a boy, and Bobby Parker, the brother of all-time great, Wayne Parker. These kids could lead, all right, and it was my pleasure to give them plenty of latitude.

The first step in building the walls was digging up and transporting soil from the same field where construction of the bricks had taken place, which was way out beyond the playground. The hauling was done by means of a wheelbarrow, homebuilt and rickety, but efficient. The soil was unceremoniously dumped onto the classroom floor, to be mixed later with water and used as mortar. I'm aware that this all sounds like the perfect ingredients for the creation of pandemonium but, in reality, the construction of our adobe house went along very smoothly.

There was no horsing around. Guaranteed—if there had been, an immediate halt would have been called to the proceedings, and a chewing out or grounding of the guilty party or parties administered. How proud I was of these sixth graders as they made the mortar and then used it to cement the bricks together.

The walls went up quickly ... and straight. There were only two openings in them: one for the door in the front, and the other for a small window on the right side. For kicks, the house was made to resemble a prison simply by fitting wooden bars into the window.

On the second day the roof was added. Actually, this roof never would have been of much use outdoors because it wasn't made to withstand any moisture or wind. But being that a house would look perfectly ridiculous minus a roof, one was made by forming a framework of sticks, plunking it down flat on top of the walls and then piling on some straw to make it look like an authentic roof.

At this point, our adobe looked just about complete. What finishing touches should be added? One answer was plaster of paris, the same stuff used in making casts. So now the miniature house "got to have" a "cast" on it. Only one more addition was needed ... an appropriate background. A few palm trees were painted on a strip of blue butcher paper which was then stapled onto the wall directly behind the adobe. Our project was now completely finished; the total scene produced could have been entitled "Anywhere Latin America, 1967."

We were all mighty proud of our accomplishment: a plaster-covered, gleaming, white adobe house in miniature— three feet long, three feet wide, and four feet high, and a classroom in no worse condition than when the project was begun. All I could think of to say when Duane asked me how I'd ever attempted such a messy and potentially disastrous art project was, What, me worry?

Since life isn't made up of mud alone, my students did other things besides play with mud. Much emphasis was placed on the basics, with particularly exciting results in math. Class averages in the 80s no longer sent me to seventh heaven. To do this now required a class average of 90 or higher. This had become the new magic number ... The Big 90.

Both surprisingly and not surprisingly, knowing the potential of motivated children, this goal was being reached with increasing frequency. It was at this point that I could no longer believe there was any such creature as a dumb kid! The problem, to my way of thinking, was all tied in with motivation. Get kids excited about learning something and they *will* learn. Best of all, this learning will build self-confidence, which in turn will enable students to tap intellectual resources that they never knew they possessed. All this goes along with what science has been saying about human potential, to wit, we only use a small fraction of the brain power available to us.

To be on a constant search for new teaching ideas is great, no question about it. This belief keeps a teacher from coming down with a case of instructional stagnation. But I really do believe that traditionally successful methods of teaching should be retained. To me, change just for the sake of change is counterproductive, and therefore not worth it.

The procedures I've used in teaching math, for example, have always been basically a throwback to my own days as an elementary school student, with appropriate modifications. To begin with, there is no grouping according to test scores from previous years, and although my methods of coping with wide differences in achievement levels sound overly simple, I've found that they produce results.

With rare exceptions, I introduce all my students to the same material at the same time. Let's pretend that I'm teaching fifth grade math and there's a huge disparity in achievement levels, which, of course, is nothing unusual. It is the beginning of the school year. The subject matter to be presented for the first time is division with two-place divisors. Obviously, the kids who have the best chance of excelling are those with a good knowledge of the multiplication tables. There is little chance that the others can learn to divide without knowing these tables. No big deal. I provide each student with a copy of the multiplication tables, because few, if any, of the kids are apt to know them perfectly.

Now, the main problem is getting the students with a long history of failure to believe they can succeed while playing in the same league as the sharper kids. It'll take lots of pep talks and perseverance on any teacher's part to hang in there through thick and thin while the non-achievers are getting the equivalent of their sea legs and new self-images.

Without good classroom control—a mild way of referring to suitable discipline—it will be impossible to get all the kids to pay the attention necessary to be successful. Therefore, I do nothing ... zero ... until all eyes are on the board. Then the process of instruction begins.

I start with the simplest examples in division: ten divided by five, eight divided by four, that sort of thing, even though the lesson is supposed to be on two-place divisors. This procedure can serve as a review for the better students while providing an essential foundation for the non-achievers whom I've every intention in the world of calling "former non-achievers" in the very near future!

A wee bit of humor at the outset of a lesson always serves as a tension breaker and psychological lubricant. (Example: Okay, beautiful people, let's make believe that tomorrow morning I feel like Santa Claus and come to class with an enormous sack containing 16,493 M & Ms, to be shared equally by all twenty-eight of you kids. Who can tell me how to find out how many M & Ms each of you will receive?) This approach, besides being lighthearted, gives the kids a chance to put the concept of division into practice right from the start.

With the multiplication tables staring each child in the face, the steps involved in division are listed on the board:

divide, multiply, subtract, bring down, start all over again. The kids recite these steps a few times before being shown on the board precisely how these steps will enable them to come up with the answer to a division example. Certainly some kids will learn faster than others, and surely a few will start losing interest because they've become accustomed to quitting if success isn't instant. That's okay, too. I'm supposed to be a pro and it's my job to be patient and persistent. It's important for me to remember that, in the past, non-achievers may have heard encouraging comments yet failed because it wasn't easy to get out of a groove that was comfortable, though painful.

Picking volunteers to work out examples while I put the answers on the board for all to see has been my favorite method of mass instruction. At a certain point, when I feel enough time has been spent on demonstrations, several examples are written on the board for all the students to do. It is made known, with as much conviction in my voice as I can muster up, that everyone *will* succeed in learning what's being taught. I also state that some will take longer than others, but *all* will learn—guaranteed—no ifs, buts, or maybes. This last statement has been responsible for some amusing looks from children who'd been chronic failures, their eyes seeming to say, Wanna bet?

A few months ago, one of my fourth graders even shook his head visibly to let me know that for him to succeed in math was an impossibility. A quick glance at his record would have shown abysmally low scores in math achievement tests. He'd known nothing but failure in this area. No wonder the kid almost choked when he was told that his grades would eventually climb from zeros to 100s.

How joyful, and incredulous, this ebullient child became after achieving his first 100, and in a considerably shorter time than I'd ever expected, like by October! From both my reaction and that of his fellow students, you'd have thought we'd just won the Irish Sweepstakes! All of us clapped and shouted, "All right, Stevie!" His paper was decorated with all sorts of superlatives: Whizzo!, Ho boy!, Pow!, Terrific!, Steve is beautiful!

And as if this weren't sufficient, his paper, with all the wild adornments, was mounted on brightly colored sheets of construction paper, designated Paper of the Month, and hung on the front wall of our classroom, to the right of the clock, for all to see. The icing on the cake was a one-dollar bill. The icing on the icing: His mother was notified of this wonderful achievement, to her great joy. A hero had just been born, and it had nothing to do with the normal making of a class hero—prowess in sports. Sure, we'd gone wild in our praise of Steve Phelps. But I sincerely don't know of a better way of turning the tide and helping a child to create a new image of himself than wholehearted praise, both privately and publicly.

Anyway, I always make it known that *all* are expected to do the examples written on the board. For those who get stumped, all that is necessary for my assistance is a raised hand and a little patience if I happen to be in great demand.

At a certain point I ask my kids to stop working, and I select students, one at a time, to do the examples on the board from their seats. I put the answers on the board as they are given to me. It's easy for the kids to see any mistakes they've made.

With the passage of time, virtually all the students will have mastered the multiplication tables; most of them long before the end of the school year. In the meantime, no student is prevented from learning to divide because of not knowing the times tables, since these tables are learned along with division.

Most important, extra help is gladly given and challenges always provided. Using this routine over the years has proven to me that teaching to the "masses" is my speed.

* * *

If someone were to ask you to describe just one unforgettable recollection from your school days, what would come
to mind? In my case, at the top of the list, would have to be
an occurrence dating back to high school days in the good
ol' Bronx. This incident was a study in "uncool" teacher
behavior, a mixture of hilarity and pathos which took place
in a band class.

In all fairness, band teachers have to be a special
breed. They require a ridiculous amount of patience and
perseverance, plus an ability to tolerate previously unheard
of combinations of raucous, atrocious sounds. Any band
teacher who is able to retain a semblance of sanity and a
love of music certainly doesn't have his students to thank!
It isn't difficult, furthermore, to imagine teachers of instrumental music developing numerous odd twitches and neu-
roses associated with persecution complexes.

Anyway, the setting is a band room. Approximately a
dozen kids are warming up their instruments, preparing to
assassinate an innocent melody. Because this is a group of
beginners, the sounds being produced are especially nerve-
racking. Our teacher, an older man, has a harried look about
him. His voice is oftentimes strident, his patience reduced
to the bare minimum needed for survival. On his face is an
expression that seems to say: Why me? What did I ever do
to deserve this?

Suddenly it happens—and who knows what precipitates
it!; our teacher goes bananas. He starts screaming at us at
the top of his lungs, which is pretty much the normal state of
affairs. Except this time, the angry words are issuing forth
so rapidly and forcefully that his false teeth pop out of his
mouth. Miraculously, or through extremely good fortune,
he is able to prevent the dentures from escaping completely
from his mouth, and somehow adroitly slips them back into
place, at least partially saving face. I've often wondered
what would have happened if he'd failed to catch his false

teeth and they'd landed on the floor. Suffice it to say that the poor man must have switched to a more efficient denture adhesive, because his teeth always managed to remain firmly implanted in his mouth throughout all the many losses of cool that occurred later on.

If someone were to ask the members of my sixth grade class of 1966–67 to name an incident, the memory of which has remained with them over the years, there's an excellent chance they'd mention the time their teacher made like Mt. St. Helens and blew his top, but good! True, there were no teeth flying around, but the scene was, nevertheless, explosive enough to be most memorable.

I put on this demonstration of unrestrained ire just before the close of the school year. Not only was it asinine; it was, to say the least, uncalled for. That year, my class included a small group of kids who'd specialized in grumbling and groaning over assignments that didn't meet with their approval. For example, the idea of written classwork was generally unacceptable to them. Such an assignment was usually greeted with long-suffering groans. These sounds were not loud, but they were there for me to hear.

Now, each of us has a pet peeve, and this periodic complaining happened to be mine. I simply didn't need it. But instead of going all out to correct this matter from the very beginning, I just let it more or less ride, not realizing how much it was getting my goat. By the end of the year, much resentment had built up in me. The time had become "right" to unload some of it.

The setting: It's close to lunch time. There are only a few minutes left to squeeze in a story that I feel can't miss being appreciated, a sort of "antipasto." I begin to read, at the same time keeping an eye on the clock, hoping the signal for my class to go to lunch doesn't arrive before the story's conclusion. Precisely at the moment when the tale reaches its climax, the lunch messenger interrupts me. Time to go to lunch. That takes care of the dramatic effect I had hoped to achieve. I decide to finish the story anyway, but The Groaners put a stop to that by groaning very audibly ... and grumpily. They want food ... and *now!*

All the resentment that has been building up inside me throughout the year can't be contained any longer, so I explode. The book I'm reading from gets slammed to the floor, my desk is suddenly cleared of whatever rests on it, and my voice can be heard all the way to the moon. "Go ahead, go to lunch," I holler at my stunned class, as I march directly to the office to request a substitute for the afternoon. For further dramatic impact, I'm surprised I didn't add: You'll be the death of me yet! or some equally self-piteous expression.

Upon returning to class, following an afternoon of wallowing in self-pity, an apology for my idiotic behavior was in order, and delivered, with *mea culpa*s aplenty. My crew, God bless them, accepted it most graciously ... as if to say The whole thing's been forgotten already.

Whenever I recall this incident, it's a not-so-gentle reminder of how foolish a person can appear while acting in extreme anger. Nowadays, whenever my patience is tried to the utmost, what ensues is complete, total silence. Not a single word is spoken until I've permitted myself to cool off entirely. This is an infinitely more dignified posture to take, in addition to setting a good example for my students on how to handle frustration.

Thinking that one successful arts and crafts project deserved another, I chose to introduce my class to the art of balsa model airplane building. Anyone familiar with this art is sure to be aware that one of its by-products is patience, the kind that goes into the making of saints. Just finishing one of these delicate, oh-so-breakable models is, in itself, a prodigious task. I seriously wonder how often balsa models are deliberately, or not so deliberately, smashed to smithereens by their builders in fits of profound despair.

The chief purpose of this project was to teach my class how to construct an object that would be not only strongly reminiscent of an airplane, but also a thing of beauty. Because my first attempt at model building at about the age of ten had accomplished neither of these goals, it was imperative that a method be devised that would increase the chances of success for my students.

It didn't take me long to come to the conclusion that the balsa model airplane kits of normal size, available in hobby shops, would be too difficult for most of the kids to build well, especially since none of the kids had had any previous experience in working on balsa models. The answer was to have the class construct one large airplane, about one-third the size of an ordinary, single-engine, private aircraft—which could hardly be thought of as a model!

Next problem: Try to find a set of plans, and the parts to go along with them, as found in the regular balsa model airplane kits. Answer: Don't even try. Just draw your own plans and make your own parts. Although it didn't turn out to be a difficult chore, the time involved was more than I'd bargained for. I can distinctly recall leaving my classroom at six o'clock on at least one occasion.

The airplane the kids were to build was an Aeronca Chief, very similar to the Aeronca Champion in which I'd spent about forty hours learning the basics of flight. Showing the kids a model of the Chief that I'd built, I told them the plane they were going to build was to be three times the size of the model, which meant they'd be making an airplane with a wingspan of twelve feet. Some model!

Before the plans could be drawn, the kids "got to have" an exhausting amount of practice in multiplication, working primarily with fractions. Surprisingly, this activity kept The Groaners so busy they didn't find time to grumble and groan.

I'd first take measurements from the plans used in building the model of the Chief. Then it was the children's job to multiply these figures by three. Of course, answers varied. Choosing the ones given to me by the majority, I always checked these answers before using them in drawing the plans.

Never having done anything even slightly resembling this sort of thing, I ardently hoped to avoid becoming a prime example of the blind leading the blind, and was proud to see my plans shape up nicely. There wasn't even one outlandish bulge to be seen in these plans. Oh happy day!

The next problem was parts. This airplane was being constructed of balsa, the lightest and softest wood in the world. There was enough balsa around, all right, but models the size of the one the kids were going to build were pretty much unheard of. At least I wasn't aware of any. I, therefore, couldn't help wondering where pieces of balsa large enough to enable my class to build the huge plane were to be found. Happily, a solution was quickly arrived at through the process of lamination, in which large pieces of balsa were made by gluing smaller pieces together.

At that point the necessary parts could be fashioned. Once these custom-built parts, such as the wing ribs, fuselage bulkheads, and nose block were completed, what we possessed was an Aeronca Chief balsa model airplane kit, with a wingspan of twelve feet—quite a difference from the four-foot model from which the plans had been drawn.

Each day the kids put in an hour or two of work, with all of them, at one time or other, getting a chance to fit pieces together according to the plans. All the parts were held in place with a special adhesive known as model airplane cement. Its use made it important to keep the room well ventilated because this type of adhesive is powerful stuff with a nasty penchant for making people feel unwell.

Our airplane's framework was covered with rice paper, otherwise known as silkspan. The liquid used to attach the silkspan is called airplane dope. It, too, is capable of causing ailments that nobody really needs. And so again, plenty of air circulation was a necessity.

The final step in the airplane's construction was painting it with airplane dope. The color chosen was blue. How simple this phase of the job was! And so, within three weeks' time, the challenging project had been brought to a successful conclusion. Along with craftsmanship, there'd also been instruction in the principles of flight.

Now, besides being a repository for an adobe house, our room had to serve as an airplane hangar. Duane Crawford, our ever-patient, Job-like principal, suggested that the huge model airplane be displayed in the cafeteria for all to see. And there it came to roost, rather elegantly perched upon several strands of heavy wire, close to the ceiling.

The last week or two of any school year is always chock full of paperwork of every variety that a teacher is obliged to complete. What I've always found tiresome is working on cum (pronounced *kyoom*) folders. Each student has one, beginning with kindergarten. This folder is a child's scholastic history. If a child's overall record is a good one, fine. On the other hand, if successes have been few and far between, or worse, nonexistent, that's another matter altogether. A few nasty comments in a cum folder could mark a child as being anything from stupid to an incorrigible pain in the brain. Teachers, therefore, generally exercise caution in their choice of remarks, eventually becoming quite skilled in the use of euphemisms.

Some comments I've seen have been classics. Here's one that has caused me to chuckle time and time again. Describing the potential of one student for whom success had been singularly elusive, one exhausted teacher waxed eloquent with this gem: "It is suggested that other 'avenues' be sought for John." That has got to be one of the most polite ways of saying, I give up!

There is a one hundred percent chance that in this very imperfect world of ours, all teachers will be confronted with children who are far, far behind, both scholastically and behaviorally. Yet there must be something positive about each child, even if it's the smoothness with which he passes notes around in class, or the aerodynamic quality of his paper airplanes. Seriously, each kid has *something* on the ball for which he is worthy of praise.

Johnny Mercer, the great songwriter, said plenty when he penned the words to the song, "Ac-Cent-Tchu-Ate The Positive," the essence of which is: Emphasize the good and forget about the bad. When cum folder time makes its yearly appearance, I think of this insuperable tunesmith from Georgia and heed his advice. If I couldn't think of something positive to write in a cum folder, and I've yet to see this happen, I'd write nothing at all. This also goes along, somewhat, with the philosophy of Better to light one candle than to curse the darkness.

As I messed around with my cum folders during those last few days of school in June of 1967, if I had happened to run short of positive comments, I could always have quipped about how well So-and-so kneads mud with her feet, or with what great artistry Joe Blow uses a trowel, or better still, the flair with which Whoever squeezes model airplane cement from a tube!

Chapter Eleven

As Every Schoolboy Knows

"Robert, *what* are you and your class doing here? Weren't you supposed to be going on a field trip?" With the kids, the bus driver, me, and a big, yellow school bus parked in front of our home at ten o'clock in the morning, Sue's question was quite legitimate.

In life, a person must expect the unexpected. Right? Well, the unexpected had occurred ... that's for sure! Taking my class on a much-anticipated field trip to a tiny, one-man—operated museum, I couldn't, in my wildest dreams, have pictured what fate had in store for us.

For starters, the museum should have been open at the time of our arrival. It was closed. Now, anyone who has even the most rudimentary knowledge of kids is cognizant of the fact that they are not especially noted for their patience. My kids had expected to see scientific displays, and yet all they could do was wait outside the museum for an inordinate period of time imagining what they were being deprived of seeing.

As a result of this predicament, it was my task to come up with something to do with thirty sixth graders until the curator made his appearance, if, indeed, he ever did. To go back to school would have been unthinkable. The letdown would have been crushing. So lots of ad-libbing had been necessary to make the best of a rotten situation. Happily, I'd been up to it, joking around and acting cool for approximately forty-five minutes.

At long last, to my great delight and relief, the curator arrived. Hooray, the day was saved! Better late than never. All's well that ends well, and all that sort of jazz. But wait, I thought. Were my eyes playing tricks on me or was the guy actually staggering? Oh, no! It was perfectly evident—the curator was having one heck of a time just standing upright. For the love of Pete, the man was drunk ... and I mean D–R–U–N–K! But how could this be? I wondered. Ho boy, when one wakes up in the morning, one never knows what one is going to see, does one?

The kids, being kids, were quick to notice the makings of a gross incongruity, namely, a guide attempting to present a tour while having difficulty with something as basic as standing up. I'll say this much, though. The poor fellow did his best to get his act together, as we all tried to figure out what the outcome would be. He mumbled semicoherently in a hopeless attempt to get his thoughts and speech synchronized.

Finally, after having convinced himself of the futility of trying to bluff his way through this highly embarrassing situation, he shuffled over to me, shakily, and as if planned, both of us suggested, simultaneously, that I take a raincheck for the tour at a later date. This I gladly did.

Okay, no problem. Feeling very disappointed, yet relieved, I led the kids from this heavy happening toward the school bus, only to discover that the driver wasn't around. How would I find her and what would we do in the meantime? I mean, there's ad-libbing and there's ad-libbing! By a stroke of luck, she materialized, and I mean materialized, as if from out of nowhere. Believe me, it didn't take but a moment for her to find out from my group of babbling kids that our tour would be unforgettable simply because there was no tour!

There was one thing that I wanted to do very much, and that was to find a way to salvage an otherwise wasted morning. Aha, why not take a short trip to the beach? I thought. The kids couldn't help loving such a treat. And, as a bonus, why not stop off first at my house, only a stone's throw from the beach? That would make an unusual tour, all right. Besides, my wife and tiny daughters would certainly enjoy seeing the class.

So that's what the kids, the bus driver, the big, yellow school bus, and I were doing in front of my home at ten o'clock in the morning!

Based on the premise that any tour is better than no tour at all, my class got to roam through our house looking at model airplanes and family memorabilia. Those kids sure seemed to enjoy themselves.

While this unscheduled tour was in progress, I was busy trying to decide what I'd say when the kids asked me if they could wade in the water when we went to the beach. Not for a minute was there any doubt that this question would arise.

Our home had no sooner been thoroughly scrutinized than my class was ready to rush to the beach. Just as I predicted, I started hearing murmurings about how nice it would be to wade into the beautiful water ... just a little ... and not above the ankles, of course. For about three seconds I remained adamant. "It wouldn't be wise for me to let you go into the water 'cause you'll get all wet," I said.

They said, "Aw, come on, Mr. Sorgi, we'll stay dry. You can trust us." (Some of history's more famous words.)

And so my resistance vanished, as did any semblance of dry clothing. Oh, they had a great time! So did I, for that matter.

Looking like victims of a shipwreck, the kids got some weird looks upon returning to Freedom School at noon. At least they did have something pleasant to talk about, despite the tour having been canceled.

Reflecting back to my feelings on that day, I'm amazed at what had disturbed me most about the scene at the museum, namely, the fact that the children might have been scandalized by the curator's drunkenness. In those days, a rule of thumb at school was to try to shelter kids from the unsavory side of life. No matter what they may have seen outside their school environment, the idea was that nothing scandalous should ever take place under the auspices of the school. How innocent! How beautiful! I wasn't fully able to realize just how openly unsavory life was rapidly becoming.

In reality these kids had already had plenty of opportunities to see the rough side of life. This was no longer 1955 when I'd started teaching in New York City. No, the year was 1968, a time marked by the assassinations of Martin Luther King, Jr., and Robert Kennedy, the heartrending situation in Vietnam, and continuous, ugly discord in many parts of America.

It was at this point that, in some quarters, being unknowledgeable or innocent meant being "square" ... which was tantamount to having leprosy. By 1968 I found it no longer wise to recommend televised movies to my class, not after groaning, squirming, and wincing through an unexpectedly vulgar production that I'd suggested my kids watch. In view of today's standards, it was mild. But, please believe me, the next day I heard all about it from a justifiably disgruntled parent who shot darts at me with her eyes. I can recall feeling so rotten about having suggested the offensive movie that I almost felt disappointed when the gal, at long last, let up on me.

Shocking as were the killings of Martin Luther King, Jr., and Robert Kennedy, the kids and I had to deal with tragedy on a much more personal basis. The death of class member Dean Durden left us reeling with grief. It was so unexpected ... such a traumatic experience.

I served as a pallbearer at the funeral, which all of us attended. Oh how I cried ... openly, unashamedly. Most edifying was the manner in which Dean's parents handled their loss ... a shining example of Christian fortitude, a sermon without words. We all miss you, Dean!

The scene: a fourth grade classroom at Saint Frances of Rome School in the north Bronx. The year is 1942. The room consists of five rows, with an average of eight desks per row. Each desk is occupied by a boy wearing blue trousers, a white shirt, and a blue tie. So far so good. Directing the class is a nun belonging to the Presentation Order. This is also good. These nuns can really teach. Seated in the very first seat in the first row is an extremely bright-eyed, bushy-tailed, happy ten-year-old whose grades on his last report card averaged 99 3/4. Directly behind him in seat number two is another crackerjack student, latest average, 99 1/2.

In the second row, seated in the fifth seat, is Robert Sorgi, who has recently brought home a report card showing a 96 average ... not too shabby in any league. Yet as thirteenth in a class of forty, he feels excluded from that charmed circle that is restricted, primarily, to the top three. This is bad. Not even on one occasion has he been honored to serve as messenger (a privilege considered to be a very real sign of teacher approval).

If Robert, better known to his teacher as Sorgi, feels left out, just imagine what the poor kid seated forlornly in the last seat, last row, thinks of himself! He is, in a manner of speaking, an "untouchable," and chances are that his self-image as a loser will be perpetuated, year in, year out.

This unintentionally-created caste system was to affect me deeply in later years. In fact, I can remember lying in bed one night thinking that if I ever chose teaching as a career, the atmosphere I'd create would be one of comfort and warmth. (At the time, *love* was a corny word but I believe that's the word that would have best described what I had in mind.) There'd be no such thing as an "Order of the Intellectually Elite" or "untouchables," either intentionally or unintentionally. Each child, regardless of his or her scholastic history, would be eligible to *earn* recognition. Thus, the perennial losers and those who'd spent their young lives lost in the crowd would stand a chance to achieve status as winners.

In the past, prizes in school had been limited to the most brilliant scholars. With enlightenment came rewards for improvement. This, to my way of thinking, was a giant step in the right direction. Now another segment of the school population had a chance at recognition, an opportunity to shine and know the feeling of self-worth. Yet, I felt the greatest portion of the kids, the average Janes and Joes, were being excluded. Since when did conscientious C students, who were working their hardest, year in and year out, ever qualify for awards? I believed that withholding recognition from these average kids wasn't fair. I hasten to add that I do not think that every single child should automatically receive an award simply for breathing!

I'll always remember the 1967–68 school year as The Year Santa Claus Came to Town, workshop and all. The prizes I gave for scholastic achievement weren't medals. In place of medals, each winner received a balsa model airplane that I'd built. Working into the wee hours of the morning, goodness knows how much time I put in at "Santa's Workshop." On a few mornings I felt thoroughly spent and woozy.

These models, with wings up to three feet in length, didn't come cheap. By the time I'd given away a dozen or so of them, there wasn't much spare change left in my pockets.

Regardless of whether an award was for top grades, great improvement, or steady work, all prizewinners received models of equal value. This arrangement gave me real joy, for now there were no favored groups.

I've always gotten a big kick out of the expression that begins with: As every schoolboy knows ...

As every schoolboy knows, Columbus discovered America. As every schoolboy knows, George Washington was the first president.

This expression has got to be one of the world's greatest examples of unwarranted optimism. I'll wager that there are thousands of schoolboys who aren't aware of either of these facts. And I doubt that every schoolgirl possesses this knowledge! What virtually all kids do possess in generous amounts is honesty. Coupled with honesty, some children have an innate ability to really hit the nail on the head.

I will never forget the brilliant remark made by Ken Gaines, an unforgettable kid if ever there was one. During a class discussion on the merits of creationism versus evolution, I'd asked the following question: "If mankind evolved from monkeys, then why are there still monkeys roaming around? Why didn't all of them develop into human beings?"

I was quite anxious to hear some interesting and provocative feedback. It wasn't long in coming. Ken's response was most surprising and nearly floored me. His response went like this: "I think that all monkeys didn't become human beings because God didn't want to punish *all* the monkeys!" So much for Ken's opinion of mankind. As I mentioned previously, 1968 was a heavy year.

Just recently one of my fourth graders, a beautiful little guy named Doug Knoben, echoed the same refrain. We were in the midst of a discussion on wild animals, which I'd referred to several times as "beasts." This apparently didn't sit too well with Dougie, who is nuts about animals. So he asked me why people insisted on calling animals "beasts" when the term would be more fitting for human beings!

What a clever observation. But, holy mackerel, such cynicism in children is quite frightening!

Before I stray from the topic of animals: For years the word *donkey* proved to be a thorn in my side, a kind of linguistic nuisance. If you were to write the word d–o–n–k–e–y on a piece of paper and ask a native New Yorker to pronounce it, chances are it would sound as if it were spelled d–u–n–k–e–y. And that's the way I used to pronounce that word, until I began teaching in California, at which time the kids got on my case whenever I said *dunkey*. On giving the matter some thought and indulging in a bit of word analyzing, I came up with a question designed to leave them puzzled, which was my intention.

I wrote the word *monkey* on the blackboard and asked the kids to tell me what I'd just written. Their answer was pronounced as if it were spelled m–u–n–k–e–y. My response was: "If m–o–n–k–e–y is pronounced as though it were spelled m–u–n–k–e–y, why shouldn't d–o–n–k–e–y rhyme with it and be pronounced as if it were spelled d–u–n–k–e–y?"

At that point both the kids and I were completely confused. For the sake of harmony, I eventually trained myself to use the standard non–New York pronunciation for *donkey: dängkee.*

While on the subject of linguistics, my favorite tease has, for many years, revolved around expressions using the words *boy* and *man:* Oh, boy, what a hard test that was! Man, is it cold today!

I take great pleasure in asking children why they always choose *boy* or *man* in preference to *girl* or *woman.* Whenever I suggest that it would be a great step in the direction of variety to make use of the words *girl* and *woman,* as in Oh, girl, is that a nice car! or Woman, what a tall tree!, they never seem to take me seriously, always looking at each other and giggling.

There's no question about it, I must be a glutton for punishment, for once again, my class and I chose to plunge into that messiest of projects: construction of an adobe house, within the confines of a classroom. One objective was to improve upon the previous year's adobe. And so began the building of a mud house of truly grandiose proportions ... Adobe II, if you will. Once more, my classroom was inundated with mud from here to there. For days it was necessary for anyone entering the room to tread carefully, lest he step on a drying brick or into a bucket of mud. Again the saintly principal, Duane Crawford, was afforded the chance to do penance, which he did with great fortitude ... and hardly a sigh!

The same procedures were employed as in the previous year. The major difference was that this house—with dimensions of six feet long, three feet wide, and five feet high, and weighing approximately three-fourths of a ton—was considerably larger. Therefore, the amount of mud splattered about the room was correspondingly greater.

By the time this structure was finished, four children at a time were able to occupy it, with room to spare. To make it look cozier, it even had curtains.

It was generally agreed that Adobe II made a unique study center. And the fact that the room remained, not merely intact, but no worse off than when we'd begun the project, again reassured Duane of my sanity ... or luck!

Besides serving as a social studies and art learning experience, Adobe II proved its worth as a physical education activity when, at the end of the year, each student had a hand in demolishing it by striking at its sturdy walls repeatedly with a sledge hammer.

An intriguing philosophy goes like this: When things go wrong, don't be too discouraged because the law of averages demands that good must eventually come your way. And conversely, when life is running smoothly, beware ... for troubles are just around the corner. That last part forms the very foundation of Murphy's Law.

Now what about those times when both good and bad things are happening to a person concurrently? Then what sort of fortune could be expected? It was at just such a time, in the spring of 1968, that I discovered the practical joke that fate had been playing on me over the previous seven years.

By chance, just merely by chance, I became aware of the fact that when I'd started teaching at Freedom School, someone had placed me on the wrong salary step. For seven years I'd been getting less than what I was entitled to. The thought of a sudden windfall in excess of two thousand dollars left me understandably enthusiastic. However ... and this proved to be a big however ... there were two hitches to my receiving this bonanza. First of all, the Superintendent of Schools, Andy Adams, with whom the salary arrangement had been made, had long since left Freedom. Even if he could be found, what were the chances that Dr. Adams would remember the specifics of our agreement? Second, Freedom Union School District had become part of Pajaro Valley Unified School District and nobody, but nobody, could seem to find the old records which, I felt, would verify my claim.

Most remarkable was the statement of an administrator who tried to dispose of the matter by declaring that "the books were closed." When I asked him how he'd like being told that "the books were closed" after discovering that the district owed *him* more than two thousand dollars in salary, it took the wind out of his sails a bit.

The whole matter could have dragged on indefinitely; but if there was one thing I didn't need, it was a continuing dispute. So good-bye two grand. No matter. What the heck!

Wasn't I supposed to end up a millionaire? What would a "measly" two thousand dollars be to a future millionaire?

If visitors from outer space should ever land in Nova Scotia, I'd want to be among the first to offer them my heartiest congratulations on having such impeccable taste. Please understand, I'm proud of having been born in what today is affectionately referred to as The Big Apple. I owe much to New York City, Father Knickerbocker's old hangout. Where else could I have had the opportunity of following the fortunes of three major league baseball teams first hand? In what other city is there such a collection of museums, art galleries, historical sights, and architectural masterpieces? And, oh, the Hudson River on a moonlit night! You can bet that in my case, at least, once a New Yorker, always a New Yorker!

Yet, from the very first visit to Nova Scotia, there has been a special niche in my heart for "The Land of Wooden Ships and Iron Men" ... a place where hospitality is a byword.

As my seventh year of teaching in Freedom had gotten underway, I'd felt a need for new vistas. Originally I toyed with the idea of spending a year in either Vermont or Alberta, Canada. I actually wrote to more than fifty school districts in Vermont seeking a teacher-exchange arrangement wherein I'd swap teaching positions with a teacher for one year. For all my labor I got only one bite. This proved to be very frustrating because the teacher in Burlington who was willing to exchange positions with me couldn't get permission to do so from her boss. Her son-in-law, living in California, gave me the news by phone, stating that she was considered "too valuable to exchange."

Whatever is meant to be, is meant to be. I guess it wasn't intended that I teach in Alberta either, because my chances of teaching there were dealt a crippling blow through the bizarre loss of several applications that were supposed to have been mailed by a school secretary after the inclusion of a district reference with each application. How fate managed to pull off this stunt is to me still the mystery of mysteries.

In the meantime, while I'd been looking into teaching opportunities in Alberta, out of the clear, blue sky I decided to get some information concerning teaching in Nova Scotia. I'd visited the province over a decade before and had many a pleasant memory of it. The first town that came to mind was Yarmouth. So I wrote a quick postcard addressed: Superintendent of Schools, Yarmouth, Nova Scotia, Canada. If I could have known the dramatic repercussions of this casual correspondence, I'd probably have heard the strains of a Wagnerian opera. For with the sending of that four-cent postcard, my life was never to be the same again!

Back came an answer in the form of a lengthy letter from the Superintendent, Lawrence Lamont. What was most amusing was his incredulity at my even considering abandoning California's balmy climate in exchange for the relatively harsh weather of Nova Scotia. My response was to the effect that I wasn't sweating leaving California's balmy climate. (Horrible pun ... please forgive.) In fact, I was kind of hankering for some good, old-fashioned snow. Very quickly came an offer of employment, just like that!

I was given the choice of either a fifth or a sixth grade, to which I replied, "Makes no difference to me." And that's how I was hired to teach a sixth grade class at South Centennial School in Yarmouth, Nova Scotia, Canada.

Preparations for moving were simplified by the fact that we'd sold our home the year before. No small matter, though, was the process of emigrating to Canada. To work in Canada, it was necessary to become a "landed immigrant," which meant reams of paperwork and jousting with bureaucrats, with all its potential psychological scars. Also, I had to be granted a one-year leave of absence from Freedom School because I had no intention of leaving on a permanent basis.

But wonder of wonders, even the normal problems that crop up when lots of paper is shuffled, didn't. The whole course ran nothing but smoothly.

When the school year drew to a close, I was given a touching send-off not only by my class, but also by the other three sixth grades. I couldn't help wondering where the seven years since I'd started teaching at Freedom School had gone. It seemed like only yesterday that I'd been doing my Professor Sorgionoff routine in front of my first class, graced by the long-to-be-remembered "feisty few," most of whom were now graduating from Watsonville High School!

Chapter Twelve

See Cecilia Sleep

"Mr. Sorgi, he took my cigarettes and now he don't wanna give 'em back no more!"

An interesting, fun, and befuddling answer might have gone something like this: You know, Charley, in reality, by so doing, the one who relieved you of your cigarettes demonstrated an admirable amount of concern for your well-being by preventing you from partaking of so injurious a substance as nicotine. In light of the latest scientific evidence, the practice of smoking is undoubtedly detrimental to the furtherance of a healthy society. Lest you appear to be ungrateful for this wondrous act of magnanimity, why don't you express your undying gratitude to the thief!

Welcome to Yarmouth South Centennial School, Yarmouth, Nova Scotia, Canada—a school, town, province, and country I didn't have to learn to love. It just came naturally.

The almost-four-thousand-mile trip from Santa Cruz, California, to Yarmouth, Nova Scotia, which we'd just completed had proven to be uneventful, aside from the fact that, in Nevada, lightning struck the ground only a few feet in front of our car, throwing bits of asphalt onto the hood, and discounting the floodwaters in Nebraska that afforded us the opportunity of becoming temporarily amphibious!

On the evening prior to boarding the ferry for the final leg of our trip, a one-hundred-mile journey to the Port of Yarmouth, I met a dyed-in-the-wool Nova Scotia fan, the one-man Chamber of Commerce type. This gentleman, an executive from Montreal, was revisiting Nova Scotia after having been enchanted by the province. He quickly began extolling its beautiful scenery and enumerating the superlative qualities of Nova Scotians, in general. The stories he recounted were heartwarming, indeed.

One tale concerned a fisherman whose name, for some odd reason, I made it a point to remember. According to my newfound acquaintance, he'd been moseying around a fishing village on the South Shore, trying to get a feel for the life of the fishermen. It wasn't long before he was befriended by a fisherman named Milford Miller. The two men struck it off immediately. At the conclusion of their long conversation, the Montrealer asked Miller if it would be possible for him to buy some fishing net to take home as a souvenir. The answer he received left the big-city businessman speechless. "Buy some?" replied the fisherman. "No, you can't buy any. Let me just *give* you some."

In the near future I, too, would run into this very same attitude time and time again. And within a couple of years, the name Milford Miller would pop up again, this time in my classroom.

For both Sue and me, the trip to Yarmouth via the *Bluenose,* a sleek ferry operated by Canadian National Railways, was marred to a certain degree by a slight case of seasickness. On the other hand, our daughters loved every minute of it. As Nova Scotia first appeared in the distance, I thought of what it must have been like for my grandparents and their children when they first sighted America, The Land of Promise. I can remember my mother telling me how disoriented they'd all felt after having left their quiet surroundings in Sicily and ending up amidst the hustle, bustle, and depressing atmosphere of Elizabeth Street in New York's Lower East Side. By contrast, our arrival in Yarmouth could hardly have been made under more pleasant circumstances. The sky and water couldn't have been bluer, nor the ubiquitous evergreens greener!

The town itself appeared old-world and quaint, a throwback to an era when most dwellings were distinct creations. In this setting, the tract homes so popular in California would have seemed grossly incongruous.

On leaving the *Bluenose,* we made our way to the Customs Office. Once again, I found myself thinking about the plight of the immigrant arriving at New York's Ellis Island, in most cases jobless, oftentimes virtually penniless, and for the most part, "Englishless." Here I was, a first-generation American, immigrating to an English-speaking neighboring country on a one-year lark, with a teaching contract, much more than mere change in my pockets, and a comfy car, to boot. Quite a contrast, indeed!

While waiting to be interrogated by the customs officers, Sue asked me why I kept winking at her. I replied that what she perceived as winking was, in reality, a nervous twitch caused, I'm certain, by a deep-seated dread of red tape. This neurological reaction became evident whenever I was subjected to the sound of papers being stamped in rapid succession. On this occasion, however, I eventually managed to assume an air of nonchalance by whistling, looking cool, and reminding myself that, after all, I wasn't dealing with the Motor Vehicle Bureau in New York, where it seemed that nobody ever believed me and I was constantly required to provide further documentation to be granted a driver's license or car registration!

To my great surprise and delight, we were ushered through customs so quickly that the incredibly monotonous beat of papers being stamped became music to my ears, a music that seemed to be saying: Welcome to Nova Scotia. Welcome to Canada. We love you!

The almost-brand-new Yarmouth South Centennial School had been built in 1967 at the "south end" of Yarmouth to commemorate Canada's centennial. Hence, the name Yarmouth South Centennial School.

Anyone liking challenges would have been simply wild about this one: a sixth grade class comprising kids whose ages ranged from ten to sixteen. Except for the fact that this class was designated a sixth grade, it might just as well have been a sixth, seventh, eighth, ninth, tenth, and eleventh grade combination class. With such a variety, there was an excellent chance that dull moments would be rare.

From the first day of school it was evident that the key to a successful year would be found in improvisation. It doesn't require much in the way of brainpower to reach the conclusion that children ten and eleven years of age think very differently from streetwise kids of fifteen and sixteen winters.

The wide age-range had come about through a policy of not promoting children who couldn't make the grade. Some of my students had been retained or left back as many as three times. This practice, so prevalent when I was a kid, appeared quaint for the late '60s. Besides, if memory serves me correctly, the number of retainees back in the"good ol' days"was considerably smaller, at least where I came from. Reasoning that my job wasn't to reason why, I proceeded to try to figure out what kind of program would be best for my unusual potpourri of kids.

Kids will be kids. That's for sure. It really doesn't matter much whether the kids are American, Norwegian, Egyptian, or Canadian. So naturally, the normal problems surfaced within the first week or two.

For some reason, destiny ordained that at this time in my life I needed, along with the usual classroom problems, a challenge of such magnitude that it would knock me down a peg or two. This challenge came in the form of a student whom I'll call Cecilia.

Each day Cecilia would arrive at school for the expressed purpose of sleeping. Yes ... sleeping. I was absolutely incapable of getting her interested in anything. No matter how hard I tried to motivate this fifteen-year-old, the result was invariably the same—one big zero. Asleep she'd go! I literally bored the kid to sleep. This was nothing personal, of course. Cecilia just needed her sleep. Considering that my voice is not exactly the softest in the world, it was only slightly less than miraculous that she could have constantly drifted off into a state of blissful unconsciousness.

Cecilia, with daily practice, developed an aptitude for sleeping so profoundly during class that on one occasion I couldn't resist inviting the principal, Rod MacNeil, to observe the comical sight of a student totally dead to the world ... zzzed out and zapped out, body and soul! When Rod decided to wake up Cecilia, to our astonishment, it was easier said than done.

Finding a yardstick, he commenced slamming it on her desk, assuming that the resultant racket must, of necessity, awaken her. No way! The girl didn't even move a muscle. Pow! Again the yardstick came down! Oh what a noise it made! And again Cecilia failed to budge. At this point, the principal simply stared at me, stupefied. The expression on his face was one of incredulity. Mine must have been one of: I told you the kid could really sleep!

Rod and I weren't the only ones getting a "bang" out of the proceedings. Cecilia's classmates loved the entire spectacle. For the third time, down came the yardstick. So help me, I'll never know how three feet of thin wood could have endured such punishment. But that last bang did it! Cecilia woke up. Not suddenly, mind you, but slowly and calmly. As she yawned and stretched, it did not seem to bother her in the least that her sleep-a-thon had been most rudely interrupted by, of all people, the principal!

It wasn't until late in the school year that I learned why the kid bothered coming to school only to sleep like a baby. The answer was quite simple. For each schoolchild in a family, the Canadian government paid six dollars a month to the head of the household. This was known as a family allowance. By her attending school, whether waxing as eloquently as a Phi Beta Kappa or sleeping like crazy, Cecilia's family was entitled to six dollars a month. Rather than sleep at home and earn nothing, it was worth her family's while for Cecilia to come to school, snooze the day away, and pick up six dollars a month in family allowance. Okaaaay!

While Cecilia managed to get herself to school on time and then go on a sleeping binge, the kid I'll call Silas did his sleeping strictly at home, arriving at school either ridiculously late or in time for the afternoon session. Once Silas was in the classroom he did his work just as pretty as you please. But luring him to school was something else again.

Undoubtedly, when it came to chronic tardiness with a capital *C* and a capital *T,* I was "privileged" to have, in Silas, a boy who just had to be of world champion caliber. Without an ability to sleep the sleep of the dead, Silas could never have raised tardiness to such a fine art. Indeed, the kid must have fallen into a coma nightly! As a means of demonstrating my willingness to go to unusual lengths to cure him of this extremely annoying habit, I offered to buy him an alarm clock of his choosing. Yes, his very own alarm clock. Even though this was a no-lose proposition, Silas rejected the deal—pride, I guess.

By the time I'd punished the both of us with numerous, lengthy, after-school detentions, some as late as five o'clock, I would gladly have purchased and forced upon him, if it had been available, a clock with a fire bell for an alarm, operated in conjunction with a mechanical   arm which would have pulled him out of bed, and at the same time, dumped a bucket of ice water on his head to make further sleep unlikely.

In the long run, there was a happy ending to this problem. It did what problems aren't generally prone to do. It simply vanished, just when I was ready to call it a hopeless case. Each morning, Ol' Sleepyhead could be seen in his seat, not exactly ready to knock 'em dead, but at least "thinking school."

Port Maitland is a picturesque fishing village on the Bay of Fundy, twelve miles north of Yarmouth. In 1968 it became our home. Considering that this idyllic place was populated by five hundred or so mostly happy, friendly, and folksy people, we could have done worse.

The two-storey home we rented had been built well over a century before. From all accounts, it must have been at one time or another, the residence of at least half the people of the Yarmouth area! Located on a narrow, winding road leading to the sea, the incomparable maritime views that this rather ancient house afforded made it the perfect spot for us to spend our year away from California.

Right next to our house was the boat shop of Kingsley Frost, boatbuilder extraordinaire, a master at his trade, if ever there was one. This mild-mannered, slow-talking, husky six-footer, with ruddy face and twinkling eyes, could really make music with the tools of his trade. At the completion of each Kingsley Frost "Carpentry Concerto," there'd be a sleek, thirty-five-foot Cape Islander fishing boat ready to be launched.

Oh, the hours I enjoyed watching King and his small crew at work. What made it especially nice was the calm, relaxed atmosphere, one in which it appeared that these men were casually building a boat to be used by them for an adventure. Not once did anyone seem to be in a hurry.

Being quite enthusiastic about worthwhile field trips, I came to the conclusion that Frost's boat shop was a must

for my class. So one bright and sunny day, the kids got to
meet Kingsley and crew. They were shown the various steps
involved in the building of a Cape Islander fishing boat, and
appeared to be quite impressed. One boy, though, apparently wasn't too eager to learn about the art of boatbuilding
because, by accident, I discovered him madly puffing away
on a cigarette just outside the boat shop. When I performed
histrionics suitable to the occasion, while threatening to ship
Alvin to outer space, I'm certain that he came to the realization that he'd seriously erred in getting caught. With
all the wood shavings lying around, smoking wasn't exactly
conducive to a boat shop's longevity, at least as far as I was
concerned.

Sometimes Kingsley would go to the shop by himself in
the evening. I'd notice he was there, and drop in on him for
some casual conversation. One evening the topic centered
on food, pizza in particular. King stated, unequivocally,
that he had no use whatsoever for pizza ... which I found
incredible, even more so when he declared, with a twinkle in
his eyes, that in his humble opinion the utmost of delicacies
had to be parsnips! I could hardly wait to get home to share
this revelation with Sue. Imagine pizza being in competition
with parsnips! Nowadays there could be a marriage of the
two: pizza with parsnip topping. If this sounds weird, then
how about pizza topped with pineapple, a combo that has
become quite popular in the last few years.

When it comes to the culinary arts, Kingsley's gracious
wife, Lillian, is a master in her own right. The dinner she
prepared on Christmas Eve couldn't have been more delicious, despite the fact that there wasn't a parsnip in sight.

Just down the road and across a little bridge lived George
Burgoyne, pretty close to ninety, and resembling the late ac-
tor Charles Coburn. At the time of the Revolutionary War,
Nova Scotia was populated by thousands of Loyalists who
chose to remain faithful to the British crown. I sometimes

wonder whether Mr. Burgoyne was in any way related to the famous British general of that war, John Burgoyne. For whatever reason, I never got around to asking him.

The old gentleman and I became friends from our first meeting, even though our ages differed by more than half a century. This wasn't surprising because from my youth I always enjoyed conversing with older people. (Following that line of reasoning, maybe that's why I enjoy talking to myself so much at this stage of my life.)

When Mr. Burgoyne, an old-time trombonist, discovered that I was a music lover, he decided to draft me into a band of sorts, which gathered most informally on Monday evenings in Yarmouth. Had he first heard me slaughtering melodies at the ancient piano that sat forlornly in our living room, he might have refrained from inviting me to join this musical fraternity. Be that as it may, each Monday night we'd journey twelve miles to Yarmouth, followed by Mr. Burgoyne sitting in with the band, producing music, while I sat around pondering what my role was supposed to be.

One night, just for the fun of it, I picked up an unused trumpet, retreated to another part of the building, and started messing around with the horn by ear. Within a week or two I was playing some tunes at home. I even convinced myself to play in front of my class. The teacher next door, a Miss MacDonald, popped into my room and thrilled me silly with the pronouncement that I sounded great. This I found tough to believe.

I sometimes wonder what our neighbors in Port Maitland thought of my playing. One thing's certain. Bluesy jazz tunes such as "Harlem Nocturne" and "Angel Eyes" never did sound quite appropriate in this countrified village by the sea, regardless of how well I played them.

My participation in the band was minimal. Winter weather saw to that. But to George Burgoyne I was indebted for

my trumpet-playing pleasures, although it might be interesting to know precisely what Sue felt she owed the old gentleman after some singularly hair-raising, nerve-shattering
practice sessions at home!

With neighbors such as the Frosts, the Burgoynes, and
other specialists in hospitality, our stay in Port Maitland
was off to a wonderful beginning. However, because nothing
can be perfect, and because there must always be a fly in
the ointment, it was revealed to Sue one day that our water
supply was contaminated by salt water and sewage. My wife
was extremely quick to impart this *lovely* news to me upon
my arrival from school, and I remember that my capacity
for happiness at that particular moment was diminished to
a considerable extent.

It's obvious that when one's household water combines
with salt water and sewage, the situation could rightfully
be considered more serious than when a fly gets itself en-
tangled in ointment. Of some consolation was the news that
this contamination occurred only infrequently, whenever the
tide was abnormally high. The full explanation for this unsettling state of affairs was both simple and folksy.

The source of our water supply was a well close to the
banks of a creek that flowed merrily into the sea. Of course,
with the incoming tide, the creek's level would rise, which
was fine, as long as it didn't rise too high. On those occasions, when the tides were extra high, the creek rose to
such a degree that its water poured into the well. Salt water
wasn't the only pollutant that our water contained.

Interestingly enough, the creek was used for sewage disposal. To see how this worked, all that was necessary was
to flush the toilet, count to eleven, and just watch the waste
material emerge from a sewer pipe directly into the creek.

Whenever our water became contaminated, whoever was
in charge of rectifying the matter simply poured a disinfec-
tant into the well. We didn't jump for joy over this remedy,

but it certainly beat hauling buckets of water from the well of a more fortunate neighbor, Cecil Newell, let alone drinking the untreated water laced with salty sewage!

Yet, we got off easy compared to the poor lobsters and other marine life inhabiting the waters off Port Maitland; for their diet was spiced with raw sewage, albeit much diluted by the time it had worked its way to the sea.

Earlier I mentioned Edward Rowe Snow, many of whose sea stories it has been my pleasure to recount to kids over the years. One of the most unusual of these tales had its setting in Port Maitland. This bizarre account intrigues me no less today, after the passage of nearly forty years' time, than it intrigued me back when I was a high school student. But for some reason I'd never made it a point to remember just where the story took place. Was I in for a surprise!

One day, after having put it off for a few months, I decided to write to Mr. Snow to contribute a sea story of my own, one which had been related to me by the local residents. Snow's encyclopedic knowledge of sea stories was so great that I felt he probably knew of this occurrence, anyway. Even if the story was known to him, I had no doubt he would appreciate the thought. Besides, it couldn't do any harm to thank this colorful, prolific writer for the thrilling stories he'd written—stories which had been so enthusiastically passed on to my students, on goodness knows how many occasions. Snow, himself, was so grateful to the lighthouse-keepers along the Atlantic coast for the stories they'd provided him with, that each year during the Christmas season, he'd literally shower them with gifts from an airplane. Hence, the name, The Flying Santa.

In my letter I described how a large number of whales had, through a freak accident, become stranded on the beach at Port Maitland several years before. Not being able to make their way back to the sea, they'd perished.

It was bad enough having so large a number of dead whales strewn along the beach. The worst part, however, was the stench of so many rotting carcasses. Many curious folks came from near and far to witness this rare sight. While the visitors could escape the odor, the locals were stuck with it.

Finally, up to the gills with the smelly conditions, it was decided that something must be done. Using bulldozers to dig a massive grave, the whales were given a decent burial, much to the relief of the Port Maitlanders. For quite some time, the sand in the area around the grave oozed whale oil.

Shortly after sending Mr. Snow this story, I received an answer from him in the form of a clipping from the Quincy, Massachusetts, *Patriot-Ledger*. The clipping contained my letter to him and reference to another story that had taken place at Port Maitland nearly a century before ... the very same story I'd told my students countless times, without realizing where it had occurred. Of course, the story struck a responsive chord immediately. Oh, was I surprised that this tale, perhaps my favorite because of the effect it always produced on the kids, had, as its locale, little, old Port Maitland, of all places! What a terrific coincidence! How could I have possibly guessed that, in due time, my residence would overlook the site of a story I'd tell over and over!

For the millionth time, I must recount it, at least briefly. It's the year 1877. The schooner *Cod-Seeker* has just capsized off Port Maitland, Nova Scotia. It goes to the bottom of the sea. Two young boys, Samuel Atwood and James E. Smith are trapped in the forecastle. They cling desperately to the bottom of a bunk and breathe the trapped air. Are they scared or are they scared!!

Unbeknownst to them, a very simple scientific principle is coming into play, for the schooner's cargo of salt is slowly dissolving. As the salt disappears into the sea, the schooner rises to the surface, though still capsized.

The boys have no way of knowing that an American schooner, *The Matchless,* just happens to be in the area. Fortunately, the crew members spy the capsized *Cod-Seeker.* They board the ill-fated schooner and, by chance, hear the boys frantically tapping under the keel; they cut a hole in it and rescue the boys from a watery grave after an eternity of eighty hours, during which time all must have seemed lost.

The story of the *Cod-Seeker* has always been popular with my students, not only because it's a story of survival against incredible odds, but also due to the unique nature in which the survival is effected. Who's ever heard of a ship sinking and then rising to the surface, through such a simple solution as its cargo dissolving!

Of all the notes I've received down through the years, the great majority of them were "file-thirteened" within a few days of having been read. Every once in a while, though, along comes a parent who possesses a genius for raising the common, practical note to an extraordinary brand of amusing literature.

Whenever I was privileged to receive a note from Ted Taylor, one of whose classics appeared earlier, I could hardly wait to read its contents. How about this brief, cute, undated gem, vintage 1963 or 1964.

> Mr. Sorgi:
> Scott has been home sick with a sore throat and cold. I'm sure you enjoyed the rest.
>
> Regards,
> Ted T. Taylor

Nothing like starting off the day with a good laugh. Bless you, Ted! You made that day.

For indicating displeasure in a succinct, satirically humorous manner, a note I received at South Centennial School is in a class by itself. Actually, the note was in response to one I'd written to a student, a note that was entirely unnecessary in the first place and a prime example of making a mountain out of nothing. Oh, how I wince at my own words and laugh at the ingenious reply they evoked.

"Michael, never again do I want to see a swastika in this classroom. Make sure you wash it off and keep it off if you intend coming back into this classroom!" This is what was contained in a note I'd placed on Mike's desk, without so much as a word, after noticing a swastika drawn on his arm. The very next day this same note was returned to me by Mike with a message from the boy's mother penned below mine. It said: "I heartily concur. (Have you noticed that it's been replaced with an American Eagle and a Canadian Maple Leaf?)—M. Lumsden."

What I'd found so irritating, of course, was the Nazi symbol, which even today goes a long way toward grossing me out. If only I'd given myself a chance to realize that the kid meant absolutely nothing by it and was only doing what so many kids enjoy doing ... practicing the art of ballpoint design on the nearest available space, one or both of their arms.

A phone call generally doesn't lend itself to humor the way a note can. Here's one, though, that sent a few members of the South Centennial School staff off on Christmas vacation in a jolly mood. Four or five teachers and I were sitting in the teachers' lounge catching our collective breaths immediately after the kids had left school to begin their two-week Christmas holidays. Ask any teacher what the last day of school prior to Christmas vacation is like and without fail you'll get an expression that combines pain and relief.

Anyway, the phone rings. The ring, mysteriously, has a tone of immediacy to it. (Mind you, the kids have barely had a chance to get home.) On the other end is a frantic woman on the verge of panic. She is in dire need of "vital" information and blurts out almost hysterically, "When do the kids go back to school?"

Of all the problems that could possibly beset a teacher ... and Lord knows there are plenty ... the one I dread the most is the challenge. Knock wood, in my career this nasty situation has materialized only rarely. The one challenge I can recall without effort took place at South Centennial School.

The school year is about two weeks old. It's nine o'clock in the morning. My class has just entered the room, which is filled with an air of expectancy. You can almost touch it! I'm thinking: This is what it must have been like at the OK Corral just before the lead started flying.

During the past few days there's been some talk about the possible arrival of a sixteen-year-old boy who plans to upset my applecart drastically. The word is that he has intentions of seeing to it that I really earn my teaching dollars. At sixteen he is no longer required to attend school but that's neither here nor there at the moment. Open season on this newly arrived teacher with the funny New York accent who comes from California might be just the thing. Meanwhile I'm thinking: Who needs challenges? Yet my feeling is: Antarctica will become a tropical paradise before I let this kid come into our classroom and rule the roost!

As the bell rings, each kid takes his seat, all except a new student whom I'll call Jerry. At my desk he introduces himself. I might be wrong, but he appears to be an all right sort of guy to me. If he stays this way, beautiful.

For the first day, his behavior is quite acceptable. But throughout the rest of the week Jerry becomes a monumental burden, which I need like a hole in the head. He succeeds all too well in exhibiting the characteristics of the typical know-it-all wiseguy, exemplified by snide remarks and a swaggering gait. Why I put up with his nonsense is a mystery to me because I have never tolerated this sort of thing for very long. To get rid of Jerry, all that is necessary is to apprise Rod MacNeil, our no-nonsense principal, of the static the kid's been giving me, and he's long gone. Maybe I take Jerry's garbage because the idea of giving up on a kid is repellent. On the other hand, the point is reached where I've had it! Jerry is now teaming up with another student whose behavior, up until very recently, has been acceptable. That's it. I don't need any more.

I've been considering a move which will, hopefully, straighten out Jerry's conduct posthaste, along with that of his newly discovered partner in crime. At the end of the school day, I take both my rebels aside and read them the riot act quietly, but most determinedly. The wording is along the following lines: Tell you what I'm going to do, guys. Your "coolness"has gotten me a bit hot under the collar. You know exactly what I'm talking about. You're both too old for the I-must-not-drive-the-teacher-nuts writing routine, so let's just go down to the basement right now and slug it out ... two against one!

The invitation is quickly declined ... and I breathe a sigh of relief. Jerry returns to school the next day with a new attitude. His easily influenced classmate decides to mend his ways, also. I can now do what I most ardently want to do: teach! The class is able to do what it needs most to do: learn!

Requiring inclusion in any account of Yarmouth South Centennial School is this cute, little bit of news that I was lucky enough to run across in the Yarmouth newspaper, *The Vanguard.*

> Counc. Allis told Town Council he thought that 30-mile-an-hour speed zones in the vicinity of Yarmouth South Centennial School was too high a speed.

"That's the only one we can post. We have no lower speed signs," the Chief of Police informed Council.

As is the case with all teachers, I've received my share of gifts. Some of them have been of an unusual nature.

The most surprising was a fifty-dollar "tip" pressed into my hand by an appreciative parent. (I can't recall what special service on my part prompted such generosity.)

It's too tough for me to pick the cutest gift because I've been given so many that would fit into that category. A few months ago, though, one of my fourth graders here in Hanford, California, by the name of Matt Beattie, endeared himself to me forever by giving me, on the last day of school, three itsy-bitsy, tiny, miniscule, green tomatoes grown in his very own garden. If only the school year had ended in August instead of June, their size might have been quite prodigious. Nevertheless, my wife happily made them into tomato relish.

It seemed that every time I turned around Matt was presenting me with one gift or another, even including a money clip. Someone must have informed him that I am a "millionaire!"

The least appropriate gift was a bunch of garlic made into a garlic braid. Considering my congenital hatred of the stuff, it was mandatory that I keep telling myself: It's the thought that counts, it's the thought that counts. Needless to say, the garlic braid, in all its pungent glory, was hurriedly disposed of ... to my mother-in-law ... who considers the vile-smelling herb food for the gods.

What's a teacher to do when a parent hands him a gift in the form of an unwrapped bottle of champagne, on the school grounds, in the presence of a multitude of small people? In view of the fact that alcohol, in its various forms, is most assuredly thought of as *verboten* on school property, at least while kids are around, this teacher took it home during lunch break.

A handcrafted gift of rare beauty, which sits on my dresser, is a six-by-four-inch hinged notebook cover, on its face, a map of South America fashioned of inlaid wood. It is an example of the art of marquetry at its best, given to me in Peekskill, New York, almost thirty years ago by a pupil named Polly Keogan. If I remember correctly, it was purchased by her father on a business trip to South America. Where on earth are you today, Polly?

Then there's my most exotic gift, a gift from the sea—an archaeological find, no less. It is a short candlestick made of clay, which can be seen where the black and white glaze covering has chipped off. This curious artifact was brought up from the ocean floor in a fishing net and deposited on my desk by Walter Myalls, sixteen years ago. Perhaps it dates from antiquity. Tell you what, I'll do some research and report on it in the sequel to this book.

In Yarmouth, the manner in which some gifts were presented to me could be called novel. For example, you just don't forget being given an oil painting, for no reason in particular, especially when the donor isn't even one of your students. This eight-by-ten-inch work of art depicts a sailing ship in choppy waters, with Yarmouth's Cape Forchu lighthouse in the background. It was executed on, of all things, the back of a piece of wood paneling. Sad to say, but there's no way I can remember the first name of the child who so generously gave me this beautiful gift. I do recall, however, that her last name was Sykes, the same name that is visible on the bottom of the painting, so well done by her dad. Wherever you are, Miss Sykes, your precious gift sits just opposite my dresser, only a few feet away from Polly's treasured notepad cover.

To the right of my easychair is a book entitled *The New North in Pictures*. The giver was Marian Lumsden, whose "award-winning" note appears earlier. The night before being presented with this gift, Sue and I had been treated by Marian to a marvelous dinner at Yarmouth's Colony Restaurant. While sitting in the living room of Marian's home, prior to leaving for dinner, I'd become enthusiastic over a book of hers concerning my great love—the North. I can recall "ooooing" and "ahhhing" over the rugged, wild, northern scenery. Sure enough, the very next day her son, Mike, of swastika-fame, brings the book to school and hands it to me with words to the effect that because I liked the book so much, his mom wanted me to have it. By that time I'd learned never to try to turn down a Nova Scotian who's intent upon giving you a gift! (In another bizarre twist of fate, to which I seem to be so prone, the dust cover of the book Marian Lumsden gave me actually pictured a tiny northern settlement which, in the near future, would be my home for nearly a year. Certainly, I couldn't have been aware of this at the time because it would happen by accident, not design.)

One of my greatest joys while living in Port Maitland was strolling along the beach toward evening. The solitude was complete, the sounds of nature rejuvenating. Nothing could be heard but the water's gentle caressing of the shore, the whistling wind and, on occasion, the verbalizing of seagulls. Whenever these graceful birds had something to say, they weren't too shy about saying it. To my way of looking at it, this raucous squawking was music to my ears, a heavenly contrast to the whine of car tires rotating on a freeway, which was what I'd be hearing again upon returning to California.

But wait a minute. Nobody was compelling me to leave this great land of lakes, forests, and the sea. I could stay, since with a good job, there was no need to go back to California. True, our families were back there; but we could always visit them during the long summer vacations. Nevertheless, it wasn't quite that simple. So began the big debate:

Would it be wiser to return to Freedom School at the conclu-
sions of a year's leave of absence, or would it be preferable
to put down roots in Nova Scotia?

This vexing problem might have been easier to resolve
had it not been for two factors: Sue's willingness to leave
the decision squarely on my shoulders, and the availabil-
ity of endless teaching opportunities throughout the entire
Province of Nova Scotia. Given so many choices, all I could
seem to do was flounder around in a quandary. (Like who
needs a dozen varieties of pizza to chose from when just plain
mozzarella cheese pizza never fails to satisfy!)

Besides Yarmouth, there were job offers from such un-
spoiled places as Annapolis Royal, with its lovely basin and
historic sites, the Currier-and-Ives–like village of Lawrence-
town; Canning, located in "Evangeline Country"; and the
picturesque town of Lunenburg. Most of these offers were
made by phone, one coming on a Saturday morning to my
great surprise. I even received a call at school while in class.
To add to my confusion, Nova Scotia Newstart, an educational research organization specializing in adult education,
made it apparent that it wouldn't mind having me aboard.
I'd worked part time for Newstart, enjoyed it, and found
the idea interesting. Yet I just couldn't imagine myself not
teaching kids.

By the time the month of May rolled around, a decision
had become necessary. On a Saturday that, in retrospect,
might have been better spent canoeing in the lake-studded
country near Port Maitland, it was decided that we should
have "just one more look" at the Lunenburg area. Arriving
at a real estate firm, the following events took place in rapid
succession. First of all, we found a gorgeously refurbished
Victorian home situated on the La Have River, not far from
the sea. The property included five acres of land. Returning
to the realty office, the eighteen-thousand dollar offer we
made on this property was quickly accepted by phone.

But what good's a house without a job? The broker was in complete agreement. Hurriedly, he got on the phone to the superintendent of a small school district in Lunenburg, who got to the office in no time at all. The superintendent, Percy Mosher, offered me a teaching position while driving us to the school site. While I wondered out loud how he was able to make such a snap decision, Percy assured me that he'd called my principal before offering me the job. Fast workers, these Nova Scotians!

The school suited me just fine. Now, once again, it was up to me to accept or reject a job offer. Suddenly, I felt sad. With so much friendliness and beauty surrounding me, there was still an essential ingredient lacking: namely, our families. Both my parents and Sue's missed the kids something awful. In addition, it became abundantly clear that if we stayed, it wouldn't be on a lark any more. Lots of bridges would have to be burned.

With mixed emotions, I turned down Percy's offer and chose to go back to California. Little could I have realized that I would again see Percy Mosher in the not-too-distant future.

A teacher "workday" is designed to give teachers a chance to catch up on paperwork and generally fix up their classrooms, a sort of extended planning period. For obvious reasons, on these special days, children do not constitute a part of the environment. Normally I accomplish much on these workdays. But on this particular day, June 19, 1969, it was nigh onto impossible to concentrate on any kind of work, what with the festive atmosphere that suddenly and inexplicably came into bloom at approximately ten o'clock in the morning. These joyous proceedings, led by Vice-Principal Ian MacPherson, were interrupted by a planned luncheon, which did nothing at all to put the brakes on the air of merriment that prevailed. In the meantime I kept reminding myself that the following day signaled the end of the school

year and also our departure on the *Bluenose* for Maine. That
nuisance of nuisances, the register, with its vast amount of
numbers, still had to be fiddled with. (To the uninitiated,
the register is the attendance book which, in the past, was
deemed, in some quarters, to be more important than the
education of those in attendance!)

Lacking the optimism required to believe it was possible
for me to do the register on the last day of school with good-
byes to be said and a ferry to catch, I detached myself from
the festivities and more or less fled to a remotely situated
classroom. While diligently trying to make the figures come
out right, I received no cooperation from the celebrants who
kept imploring me to rejoin them.

The following day, June 20th, was "D-Day" ... the day
I'd depart from a great bunch of kids and teachers. Good-
byes tend to leave me depressed. If it were possible, disap-
pearing suddenly would be preferable. Not being capable
of vanishing, I managed to say all my farewells. When the
time came to bid adieu to one particular boy, I couldn't help
smiling as I recalled his standing behind home plate during
an after-school baseball session, a catcher's mask raised just
high enough to allow a lit cigarette to dangle from his lips
while he shouted to me to throw him the ball.

Upon leaving South Centennial School, I figured that all
my students had said their last good-byes. But surprisingly,
three hours later, as my family and I waited to board the
Bluenose, who should appear out of the heavy fog but several
of my students with an encore of farewells.

They were still there, although barely visible, as the sleek
vessel slipped away from its wharf, blew its whistle, and
headed for Bar Harbor, Maine.

What else was there to say but: Sorgi, baby, you *are* a
millionaire!!!!!

YORK COLLEGE OF PENNSYLVANIA 17403

0 2003 0005613 8

LA 2317 .S635 A3 1988
Sorgi, Bob, 1932-
You've got to learn because
 I've got to teach

DISCARDED

LIBRARY